Helen Gibson Carves



# SAINT FRANCIS OF ASSISI

Text written with and photography by Douglas Congdon-Martin

Schiffer Publishing Ltd
77 Lower Valley Road, Atglen, PA 19310

# Contents

Library of Congress Catalog Number: 93-87049



Printed in United States of America
ISBN: 0-88740-586-X



If you would like to know more about the history of the Folk School and the Brasstown carvers, there is an illustrated book available from the school. Write: John C. Campbell Folk School, Brassstown, North Carolina 28902.

DESIGNED BY MARK S. BALBACH

Published by Schiffer Publishing Ltd.
77 Lower Valley Road
Atglen, PA 19310
Please write for a free catalog.
This book may be purchased from the publisher.
Please include $2.95 postage.
Try your bookstore first.

# Introduction

Francis was born in Assisi in 1181 or 1182. His father, a rich merchant, was away in France at the time, and gave the name of that country to his son. By all accounts he was a happy child, nurtured by a loving family. He was prepared to follow in his father's business, after spending some youthful years as a knight. On military adventure in 1201, he was captured and spent a year as a hostage in Perugia.

This marked a change in his life. He soon gave up the military life, having heard the voice of Christ calling him to service. He turned himself to the poor and the sick. Following the voice again, he became a hermit, renouncing his old life. His father had him put in prison to try to change his mind. When this did not work he took him before the bishop. There Francis gave up his inheritance, both his rights and possessions, including even his clothes.

His life continued as it was for two more years, until in February, 1209, he heard a call to penance in the morning mass. He gave up the hermit's life and took on the rough tunic and cord of the monk.

This is the Francis that we are carving in this book. With his followers he lived the simple life, doing honest work or accepting the gifts of those in the community. They went about preaching Christ and doing kindness. Francis was respected by the people and the church alike. Soon his message of simplicity grew into a movement within the church, with many hundreds of followers organized into a great order. But that was largely left to others. Francis's gifts were in the simple spirituality that witnessed to Christ.

His popularity and recognition have gone beyond the Catholic church. He has been hailed as "the most lovable of the Saints" and "the only true Christian." He is seen as a lover of flowers, a friend of animals, a poet, a humanitarian. All these are true, but most importantly Francis was a simple, faithful person, whose life was lived in imitation of Christ's. No wonder he is so revered even today. I have been carving his figure for many years, and it always seems to spark a special interest in people.

I hope you enjoy carving Francis, as much as I have.

# Carving Saint Francis

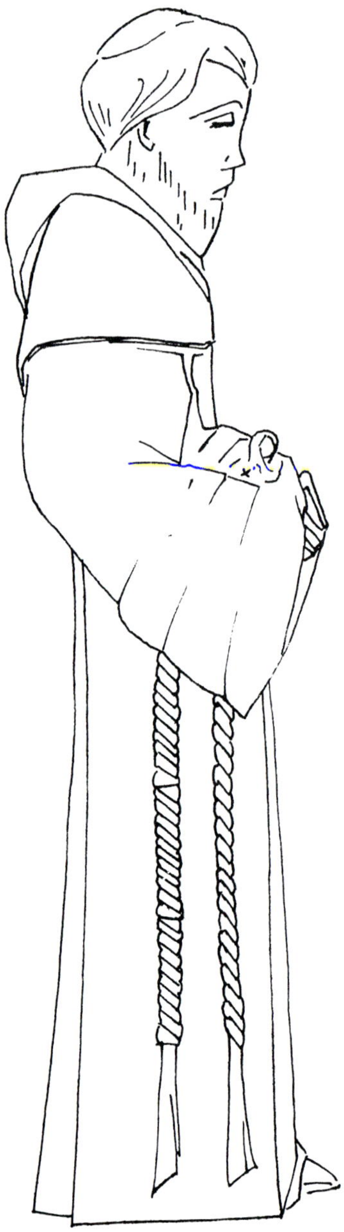

Cut the pattern from 3 1/4 inch stock. I used basswood here, but sometimes it is nice to use butternut, walnut, cherry or buckeye. Mark the center line all the way around.

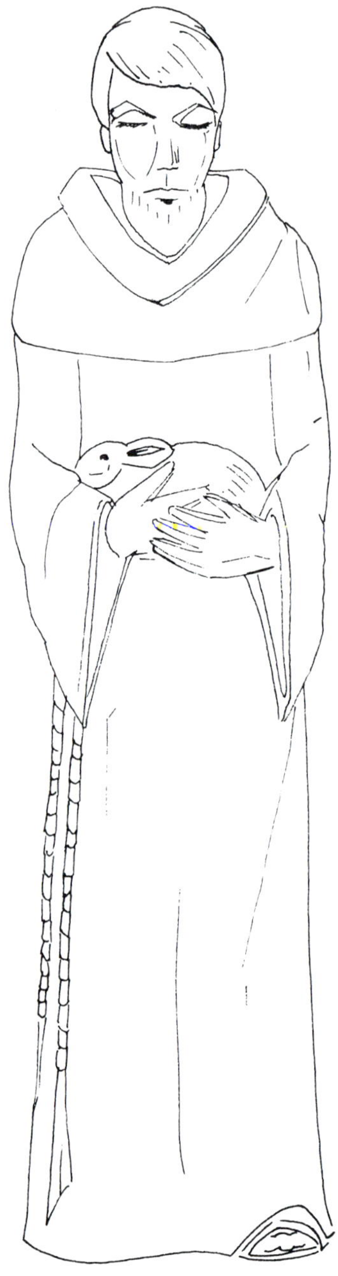

*Enlarge patterns* **175%** *to achieve original size.*

Mark the head area by dividing the halves in half.

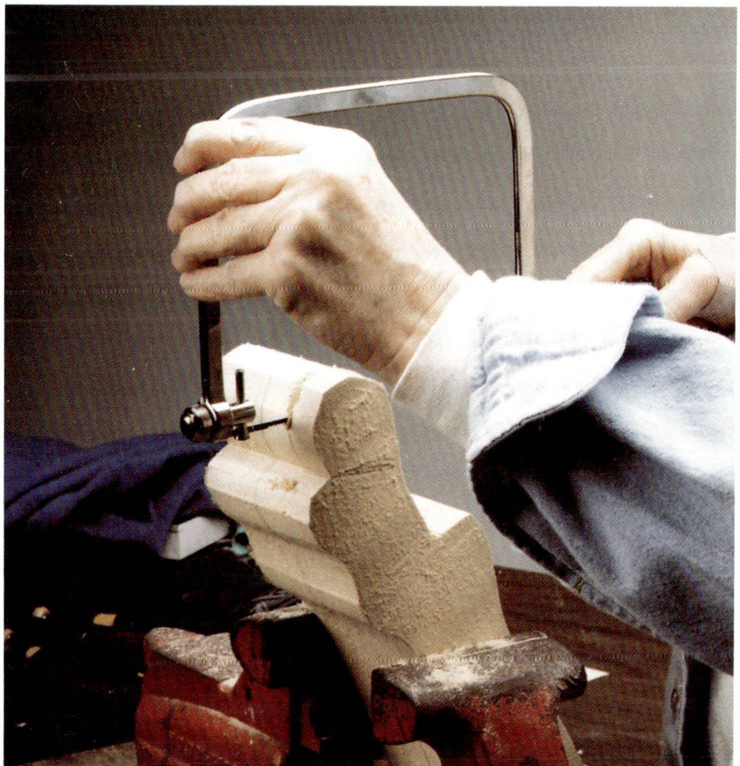

With the blank in a vise, cut along the head lines down to the shoulder.

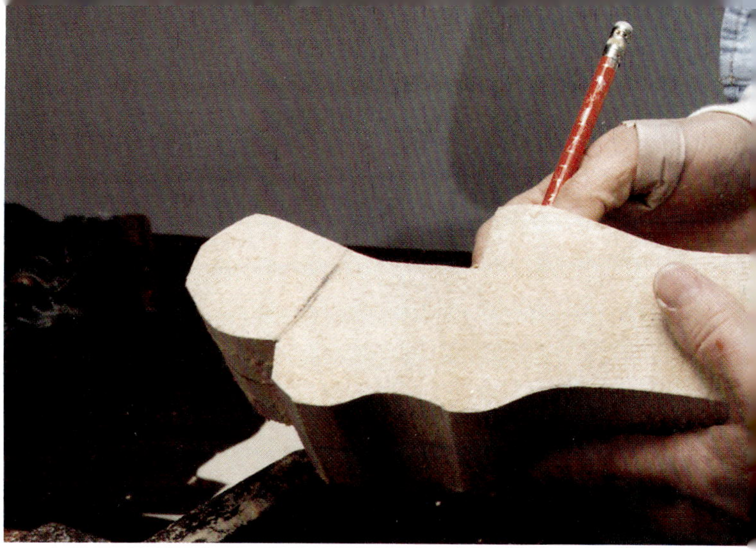

Mark the neck on the sides.

Cut along the neck line to remove the excess wood.

The result.

Cut off the corners of the head.

Draw the line of the back where it meets the hood.

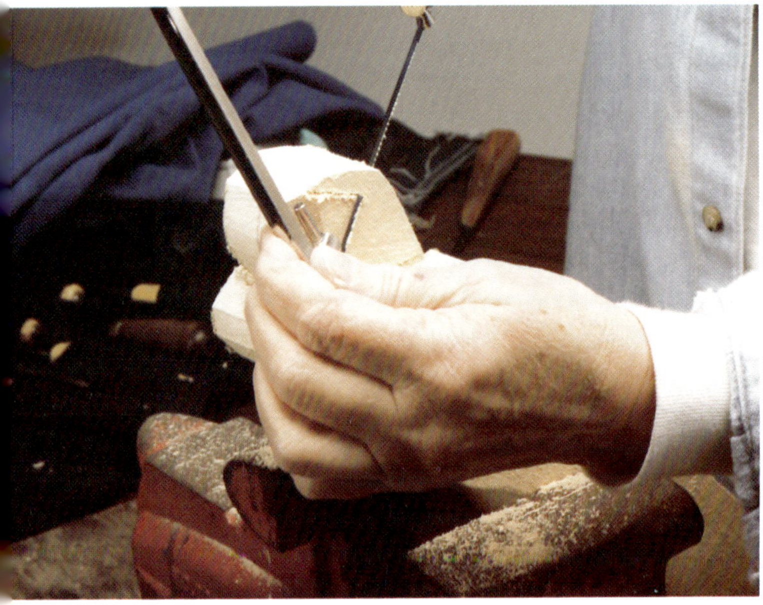

On the front, follow the curve of the head.

Draw the back of the hood.

At the bottom of the head, cut back to pop it off.

Cut down the line of the hood to the back.

Cut across the back to the hood to pop out the excess.

Do the same with the turn of the hood, cutting down  and in.

Mark the shoulder and the line of the sleeve.

Draw the line of the sleeve and the robe in the front...

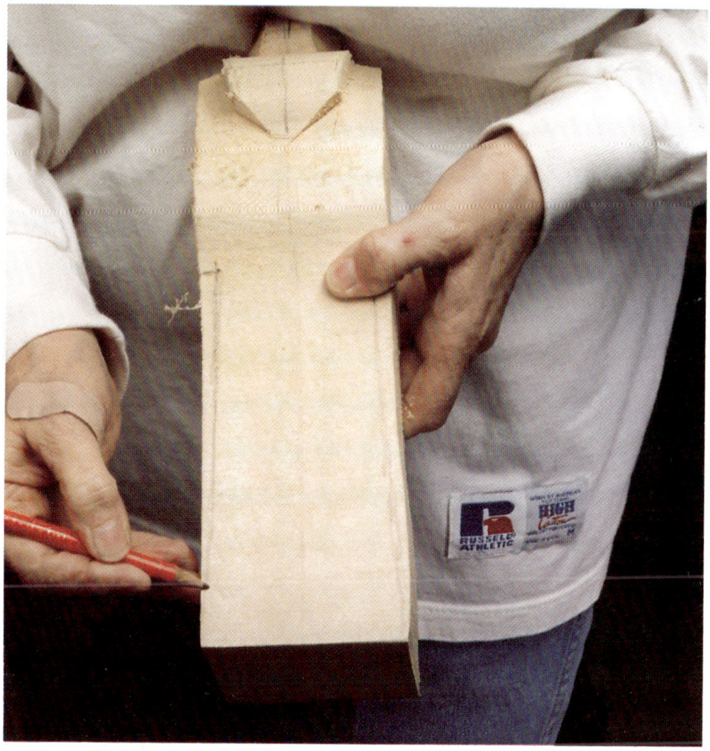

and the back.

Cut on the sleeve line.

Repeat on the other side.

With a wide gouge, come up the robe to the sleeve.

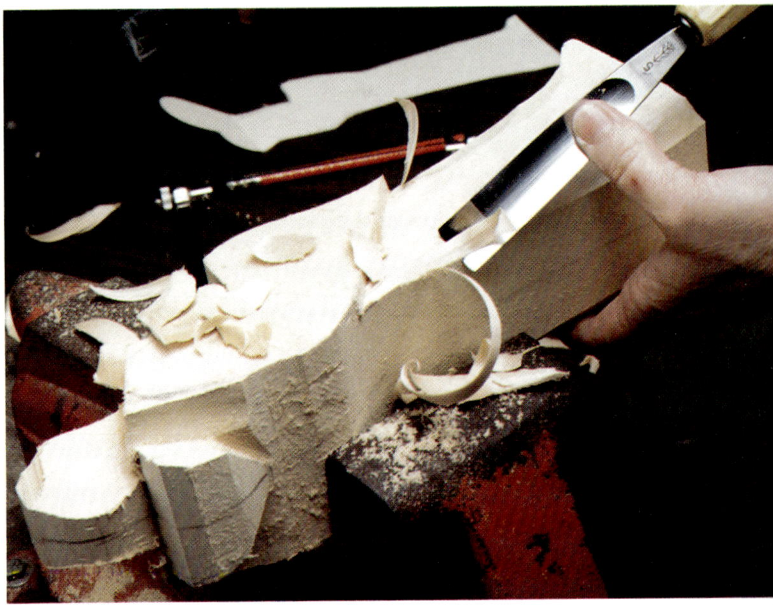

Again, round the back corner.

Round the back corners quite a bit as you go.

Draw the line of the feet on the bottom. One foot will be sticking out from under the robe.

Cut around the foot line with the coping saw.

With a gouge, carve the front of the robe to follow the line of the feet.

Continue up to the arm.

Progress.

Mark the area to be removed at the side of the arms.

Use the chisel to remove the excess.

Take the corner off the lower edge of the sleeve.

Repeat on the other side.

Be careful not to take any wood off the elbows. These are the widest point.

A corner needs to come out of the top side of the arms. This leaves a block in the middle for the rabbit St. Francis is holding.

Clean the outside edge with a gouge.

With the piece in a vise, go straight in with a v-tool to remove the corners.

On the center line of the block between the arms, go straight in with the v-tool. This is the back of the rabbit's ears.

This gives you a nice straight line.

Draw in the shape of the rabbit.

Use a gouge to lower the back part of the rabbit's body.

Progress so far.

Take the wood down to the outline of the head.

Draw in the underside of the rabbit and the inside of the sleeves.

Take a little off the front edge of the head.

With a gouge remove the excess between the sleeves in front.

I find it easiest to build up chips in one direction....

then come back and clip them off.

Work your way up the front of the robe, blending it in.

Deepen the sides...

and clip off the chip.

To help his foot come forward, I'll take off a little along these lines.

Use a flatter gouge to do this.

Change to a smaller gouge and go a little bit deeper.

Do the same thing on the side line. First a wider gouge...

then a smaller one.

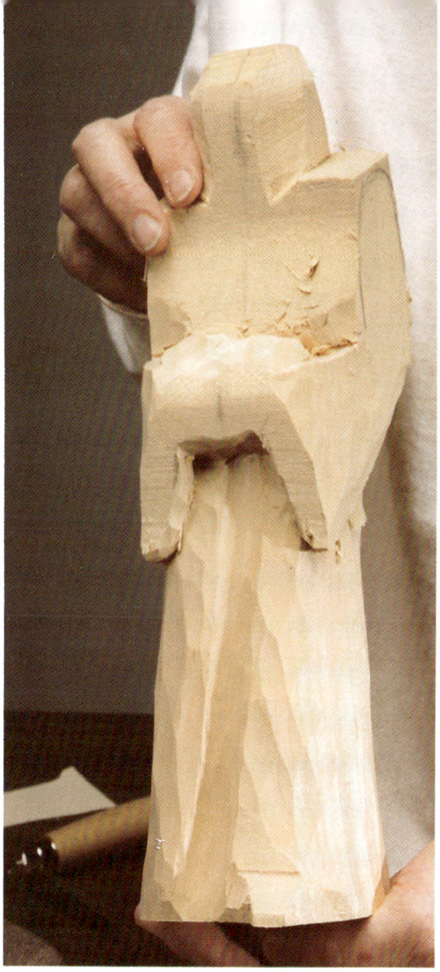

You can begin to see the contours of the robe.

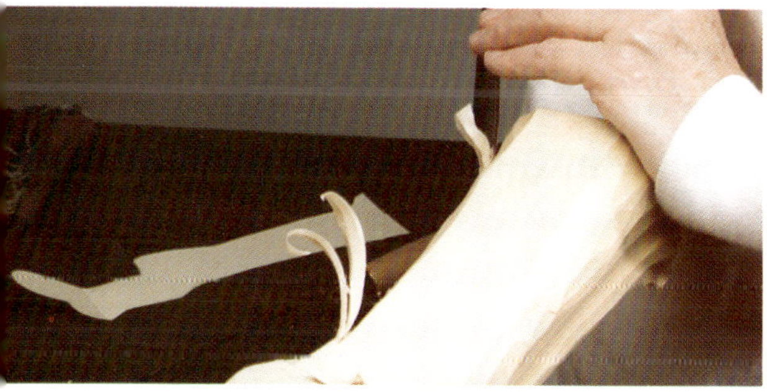

Round the corners of the back.

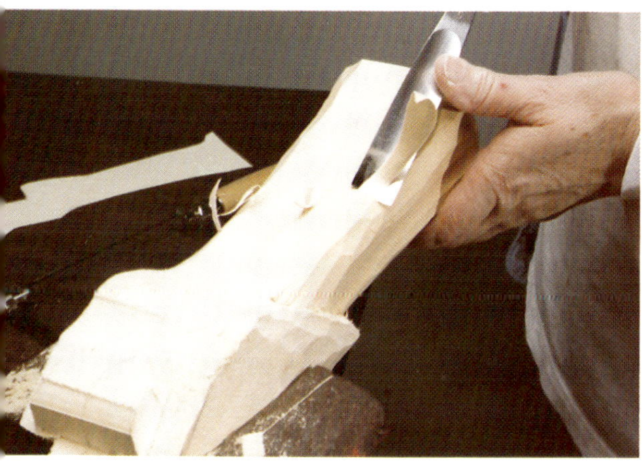

On the corner behind the forward foot, make it a little deeper than the other side.

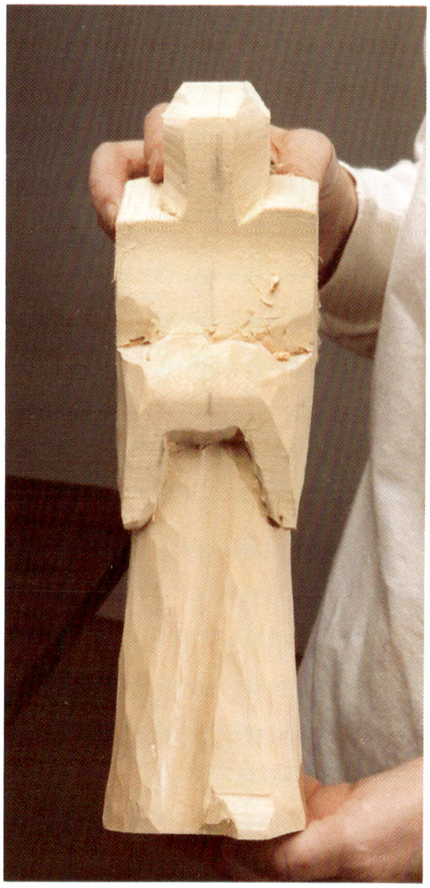

Progress from the "vise" phase.

Round the shoulders...

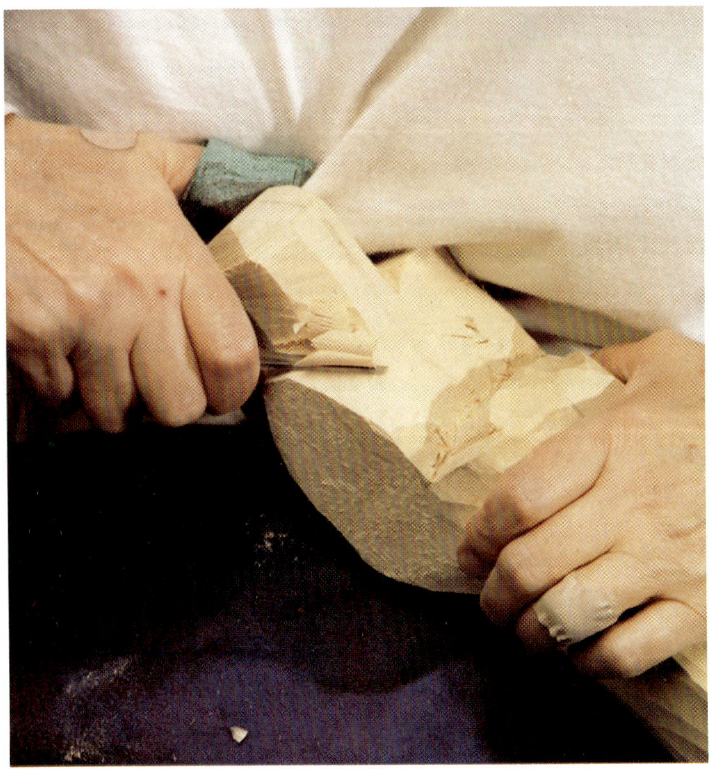

and the upper chest.

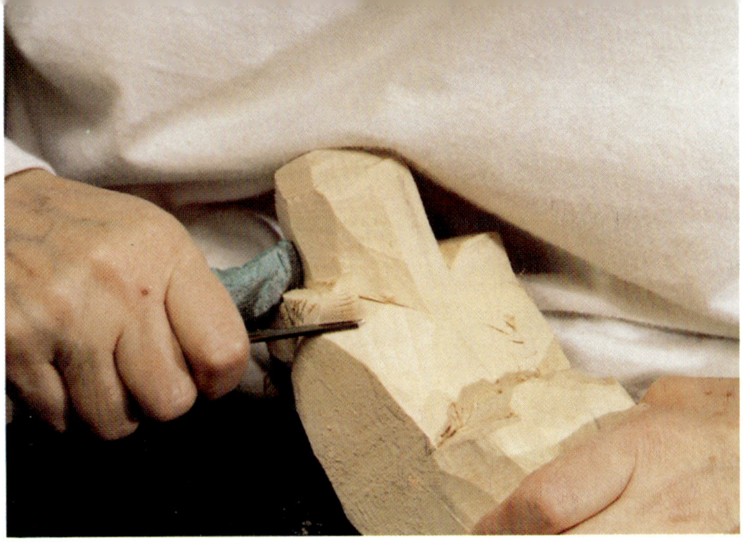

Give the shoulders some slope.

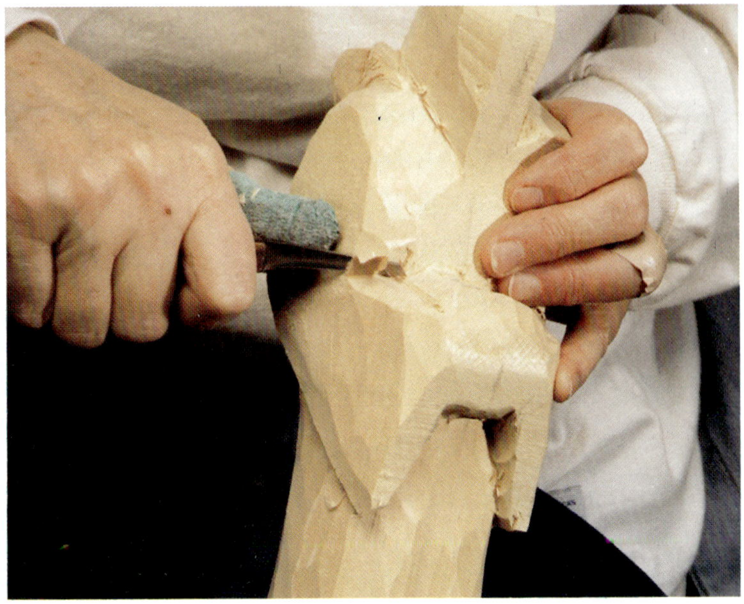

Round the upper arm to the crook.

Start to shape the head.

Work around the sides and back, but don't touch the front for now.

Take some off the front of the shoulders. This helps the elbow stick out more.

Cut into the bottom of the beard.

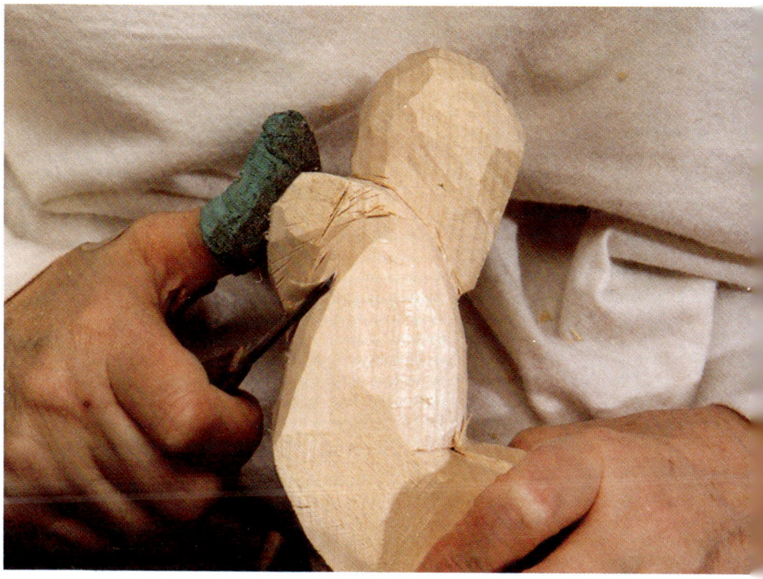

Knock the corners off the back of the arms.

and back to it from the chest.

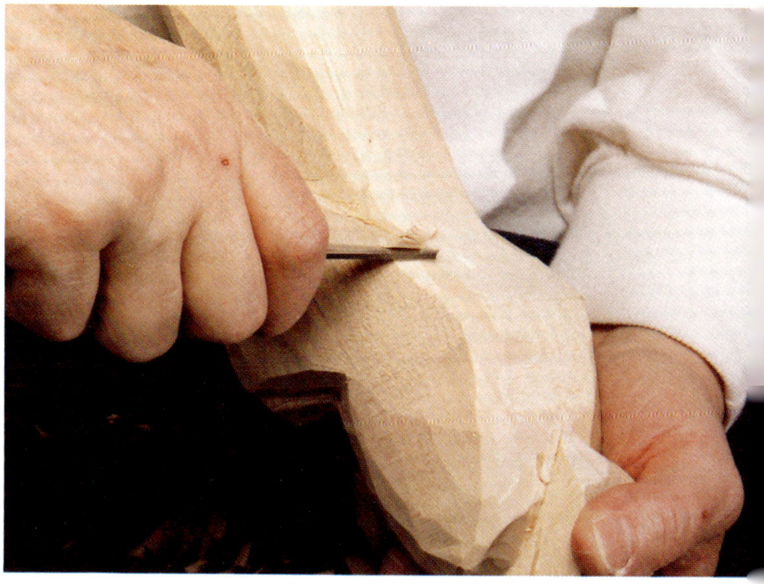

Take a little off the lower edge of the forearm. This moves the elbow higher.

Knock the corners off the hood.

and trimming back to it from the robe.

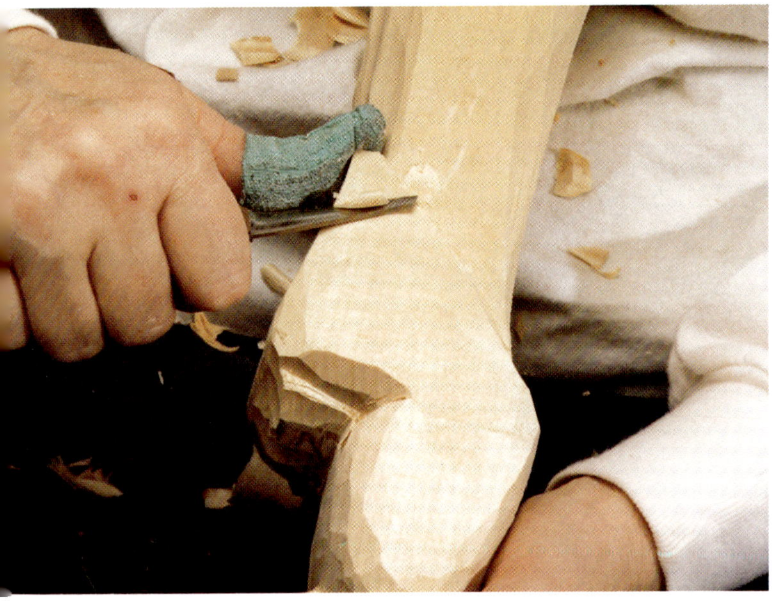

Smooth off the sleeve.

Do the same on the other side.

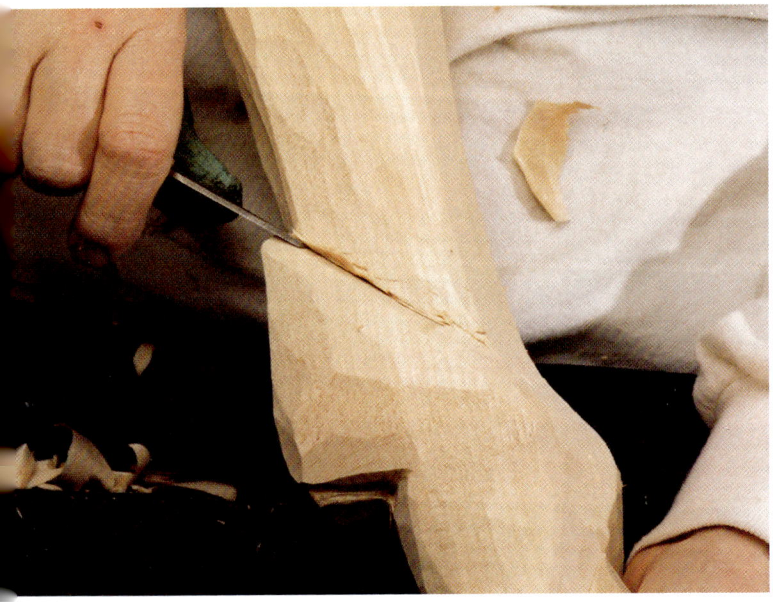

Define the bottom of the sleeve by making a stop cut...

Trim down the lower edge of the sleeve.

Clean up the chest, bringing out the rabbit as you go.

Trim back to it from the robe.

Draw in the mantle.

Go over it again, deepening the stop...

Make a stop cut all around the mantle.

and cutting back to it.

The shoulders need a little more slope.

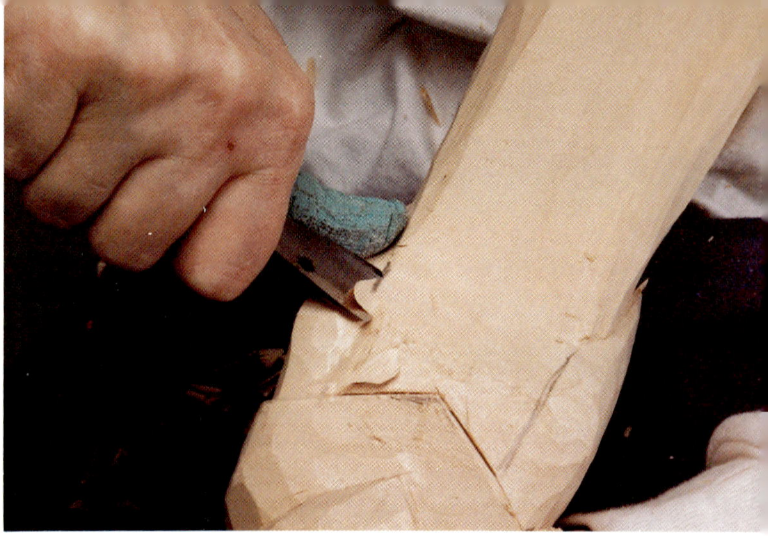

Use the gouge along the arm line to bring it out.

In the back, draw the inside of the arms.

Do the same on the other side.

Make a stop below the mantle in the back.

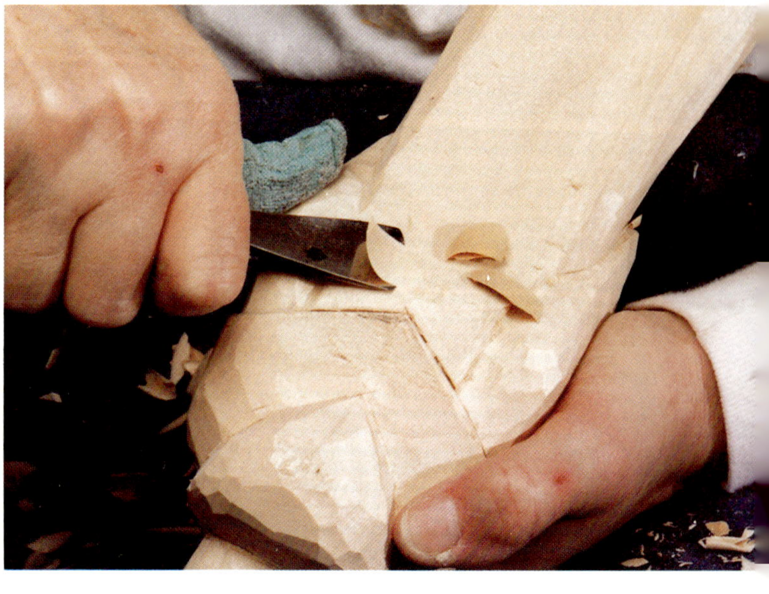

Then you can work down from the stop going from side to side with the gouge to remove the excess wood.

As you go deeper you have to go back and deepen the stop cut below the mantle.

You can use the gouge to slim the arm down. This one was a little thicker than the other one.

As I move deeper I switch to a smaller gouge to get better access.

Progress on the back.

Go back to the wider gouge to smooth things up.

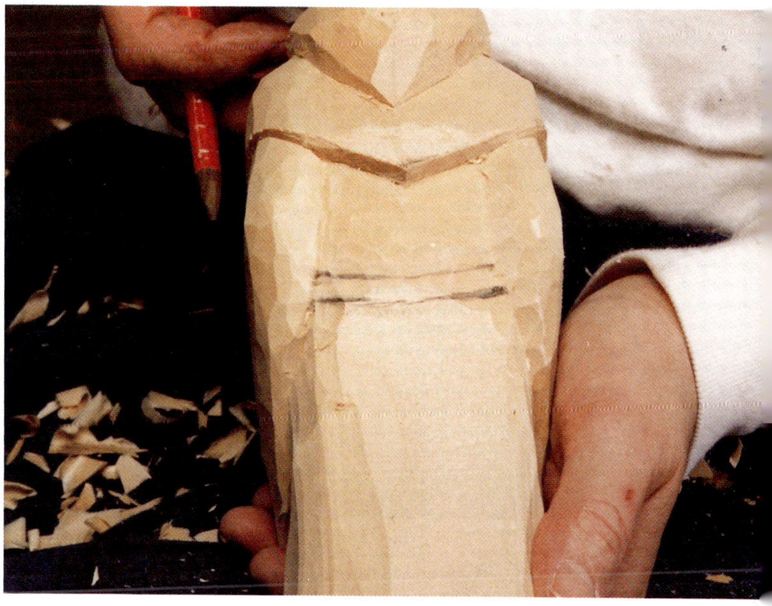

Draw the line of the cincture. It should be just below the elbow.

Make a stop cut in each line.

Also cut back to the cincture from the robe above it.

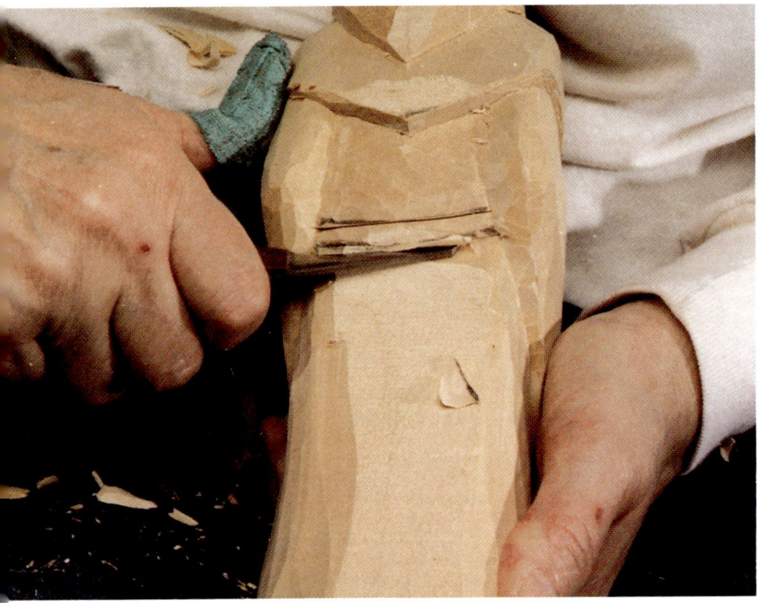

Trim back to it from the robe.

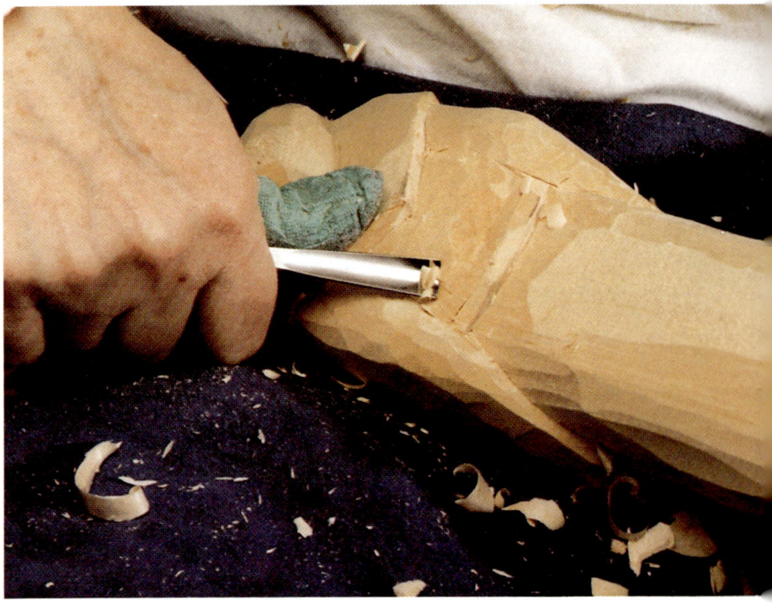

In some spots it will be easier to use a gouge, either a small one or...

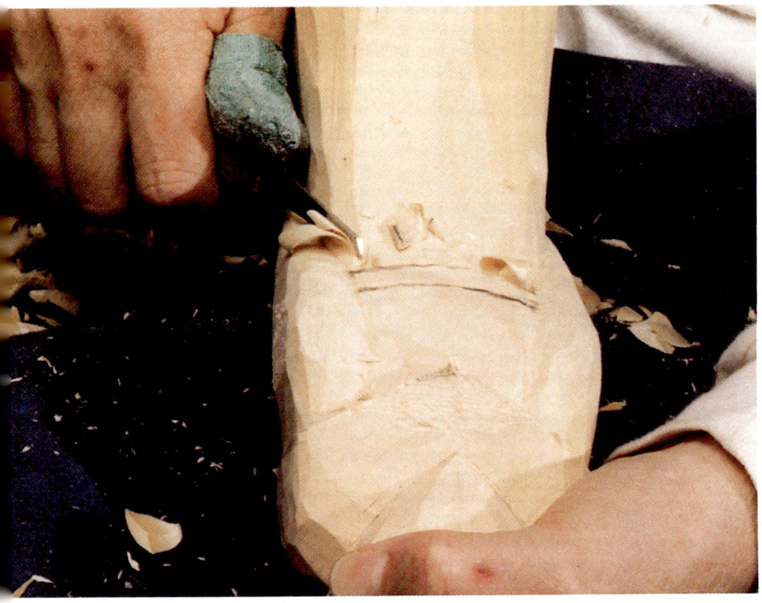

Bring out the elbow by reducing the robe under it.

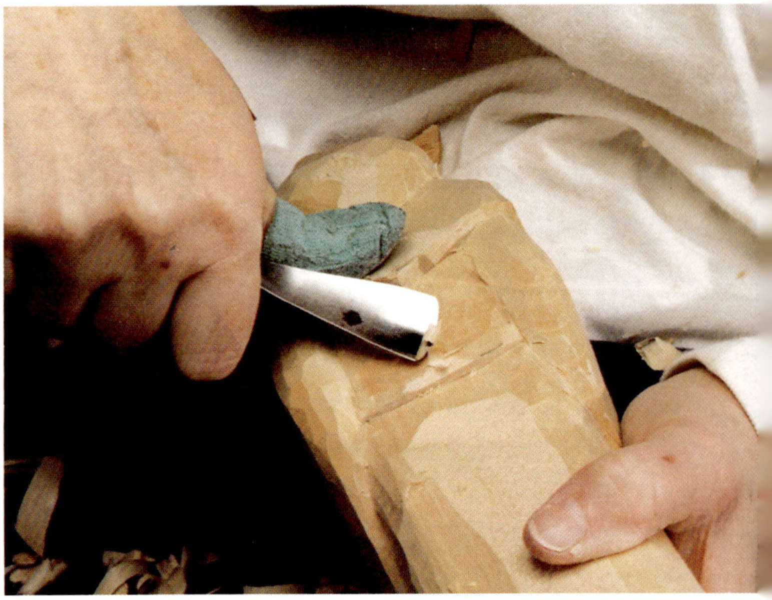

a larger one.

Round over the edges of the belt.

and then rounding the upper portion.

Narrow the robe so it tapers under the sleeves naturally.

Spend some time smoothing the robe.

Round off the foot by first establishing its outline...

A little of the knee shape should show above the forward foot, so work above and below the knee to bring it out.

Define the flow of the robe around the foot.

The wide gouge is a good smoothing tool.

You bring the back left side forward more because the left foot is sticking out.

Draw in some lines for pleats in the back.

Do a cup cut at the end of the pleats with the knife.

Follow the line from the bottom with a gouge.

Switch to a V-tool to get the definition and depth you desire.

Smooth and blend the lines with a knife.

Trim off the curls with a knife.

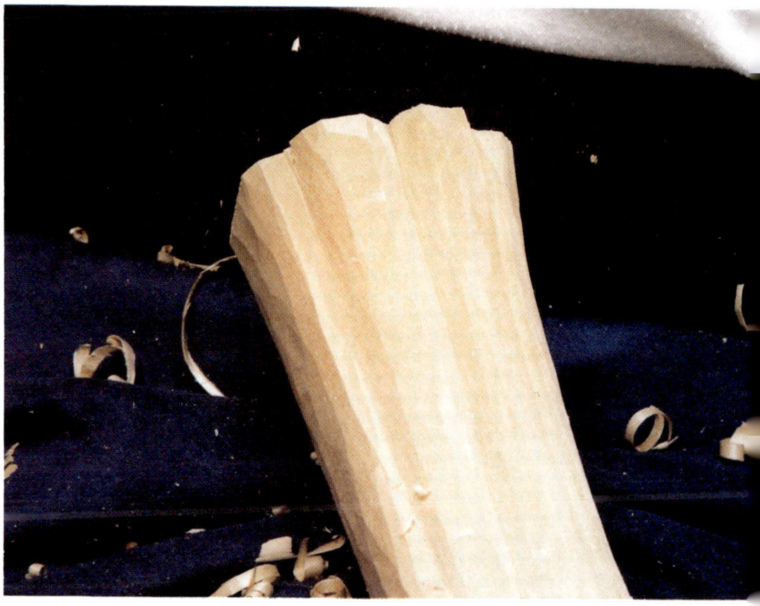

Your goal is to round off these folds in a natural looking way.

Open up the pleats with a gouge.

Sometimes the grain and the position make it easier to use a gouge for the smoothing.

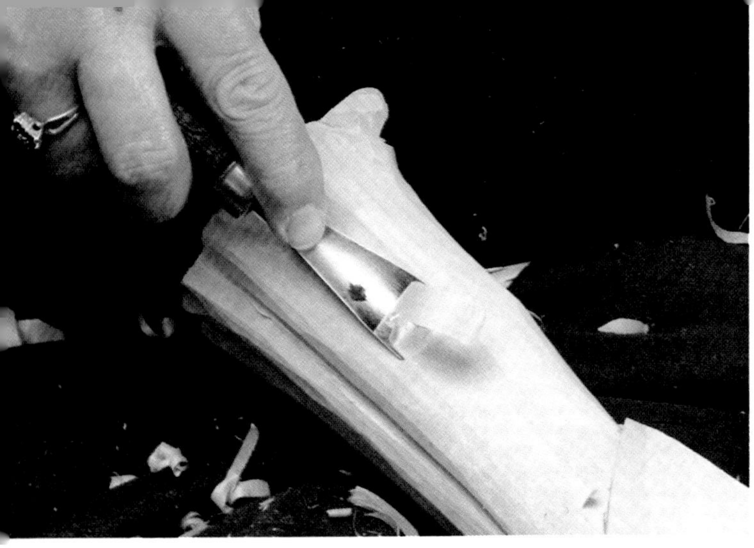

Continue up the robe.

to the other side.

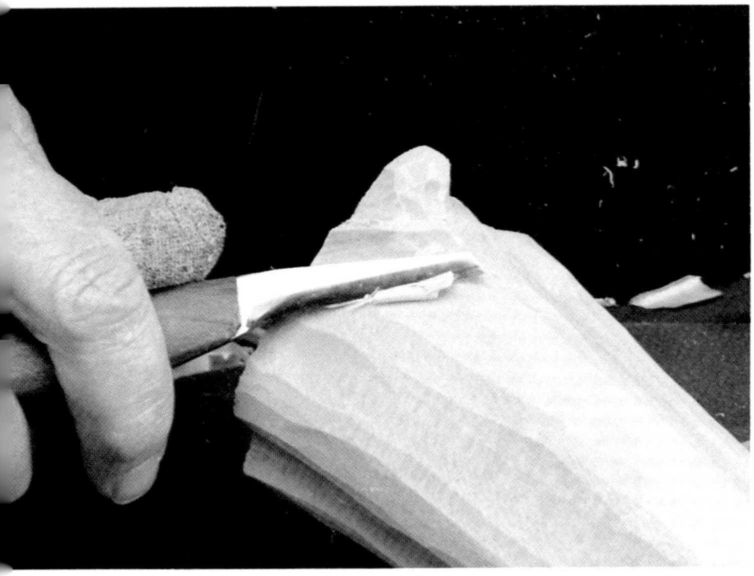

A series of curl cuts will establish the robe's line over the foot. Start on the side...

Progress.

and work your way over the top...

Clean up around the foot to emphasis the line where the robe overlaps the foot.

Go back over the work, looking for details. Here I needed to deepen of the pleat lines with a veiner.

With the veiner add a few shorter pleats.

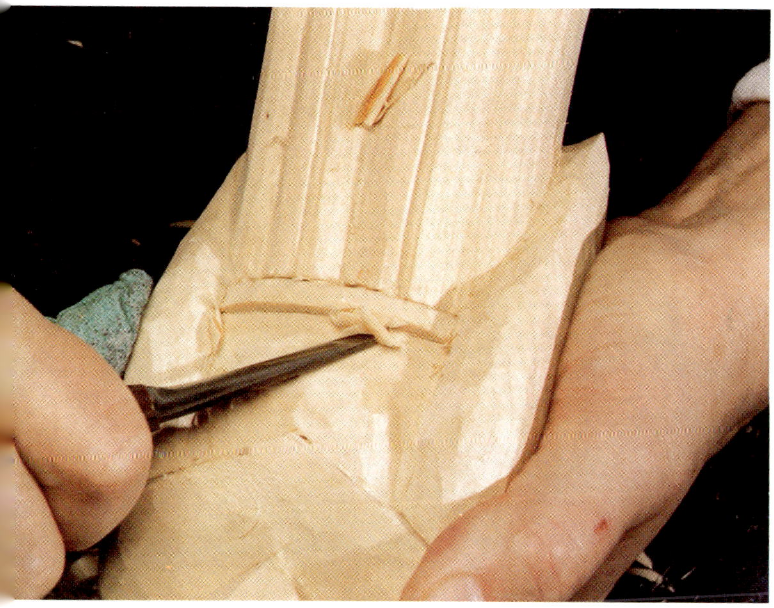

Clean up the line where the back goes under the belt.

Go back and round off the belt.

We need to remove some of the sleeve in front of the rabbit's face. Use a veiner to set the depth...

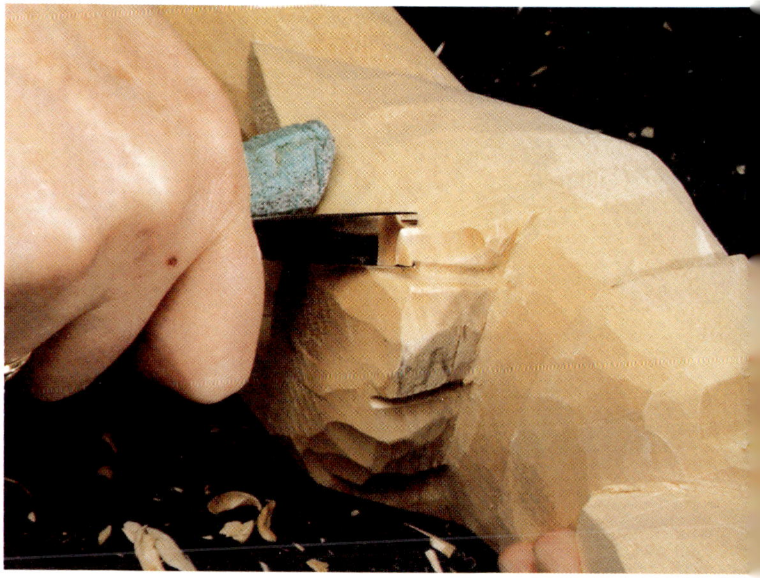

and remove the wood with a gouge.

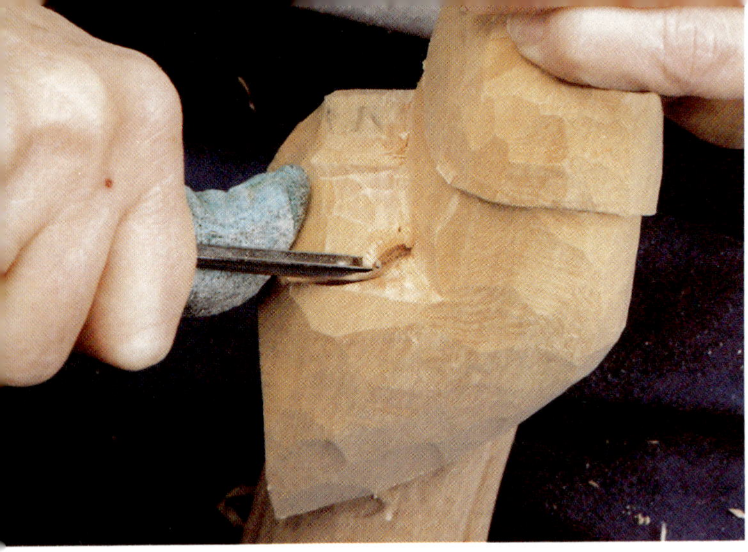

Do the same at the rear of the rabbit. First the veiner to define the depth...

Round the back part of the rabbit with a gouge.

then the gouge to take off the wood.

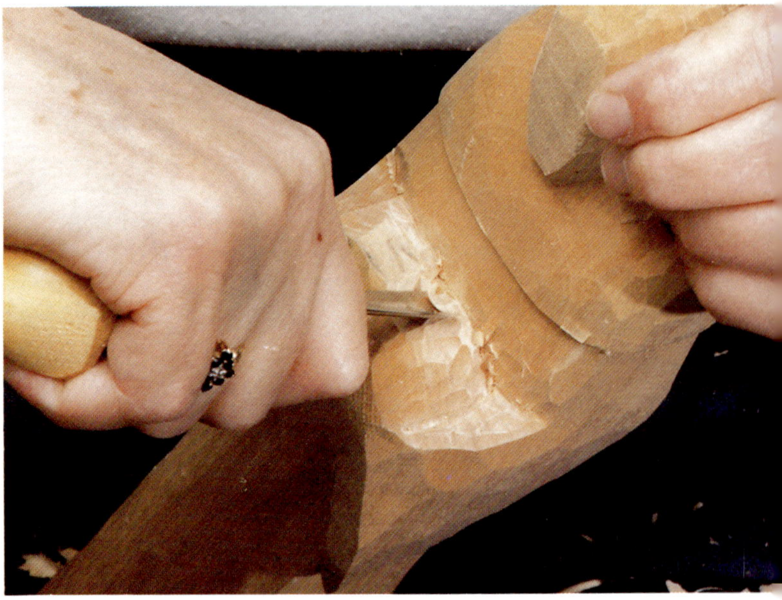

I want the back to be just a little bit lower than the head.

This should take the rabbit to about this state.

Use the gouge to thin the rabbit's head and bring it closer to the body.

Knock off the corner of the nose.

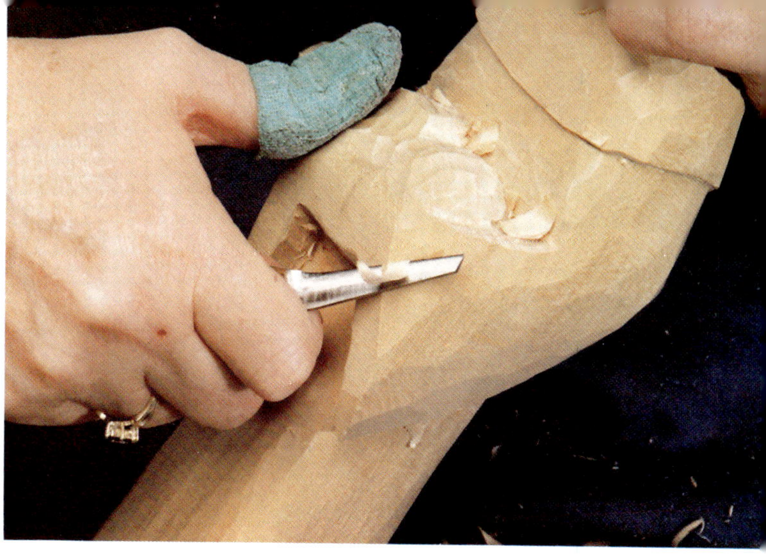

Smooth the forearms and round the area of the hands.

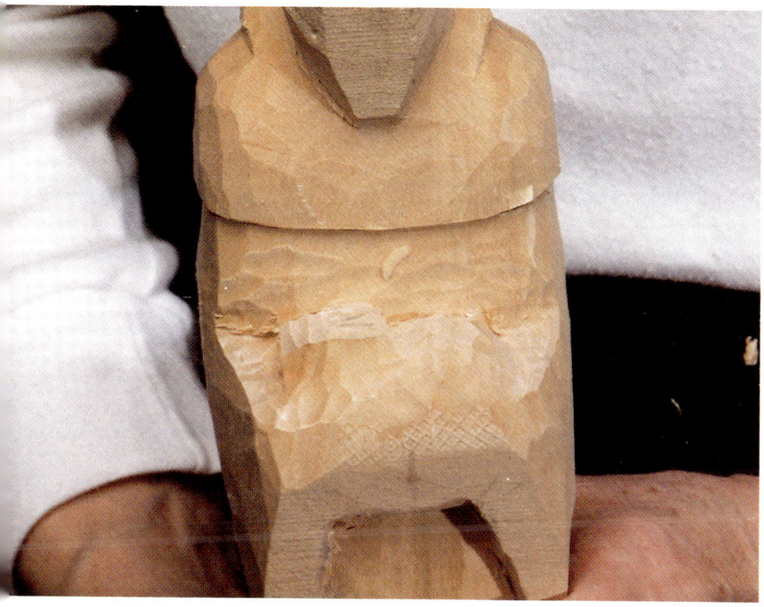

This is the shape you want for the rabbit...

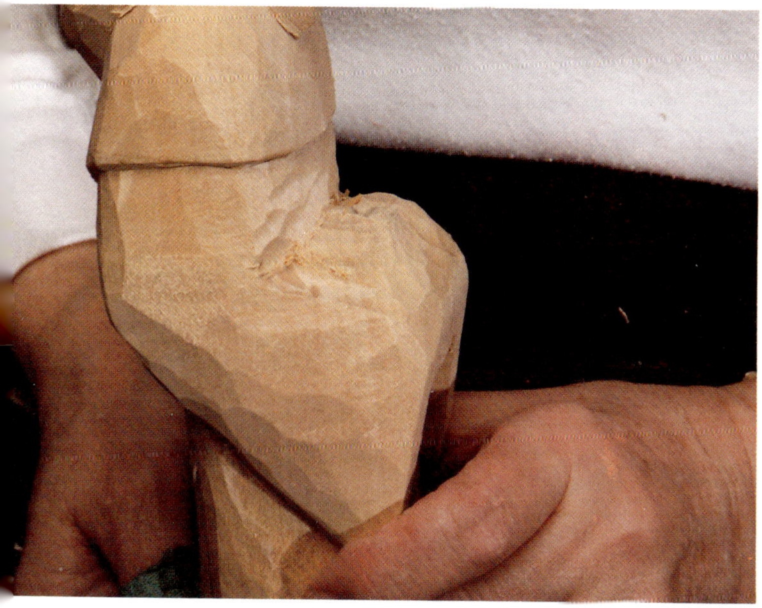

before going to work on the hands.

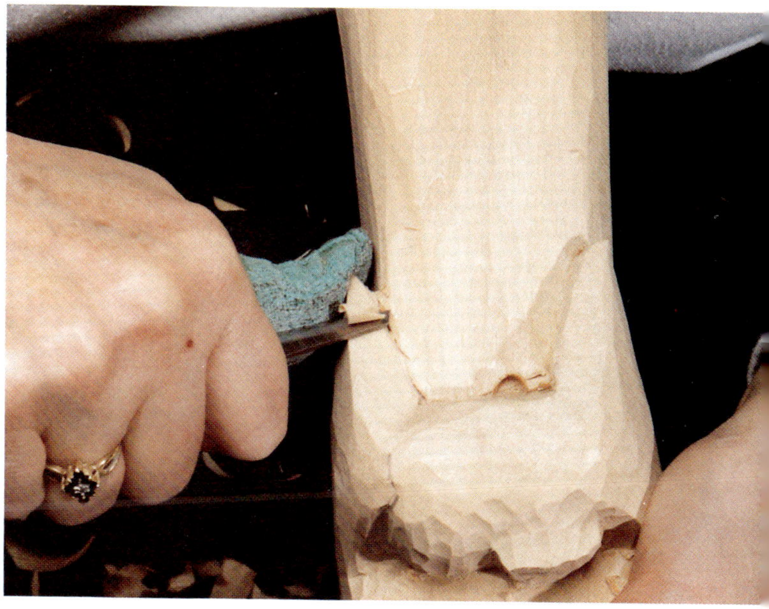

Angle the opening of the sleeves...

in toward the body.

Draw the line of the sleeves.

I need to remove some of the wood under the hands.

Make a stop cut at the wrist...

The gouge works well in this position.

and cut back to it from the hand.

Come up the robe with the gouge to clean up the work.

Draw in the outline of the hands.

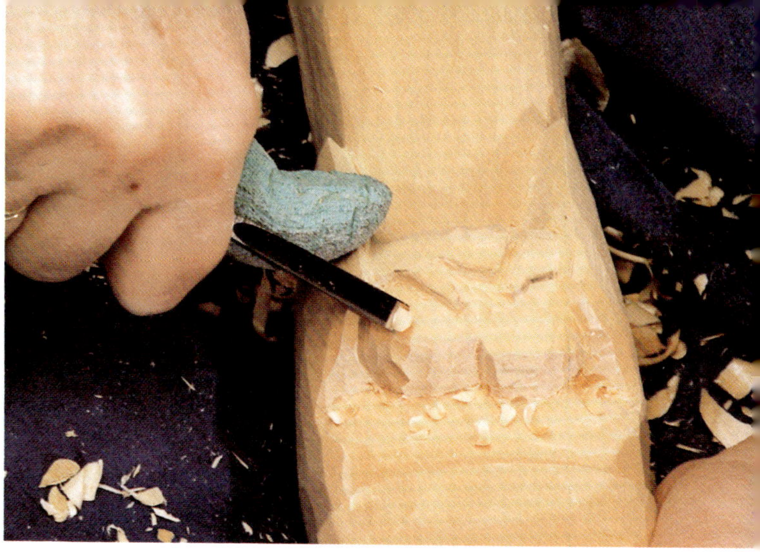

Use a small gouge to clean up the lines and blend them in.

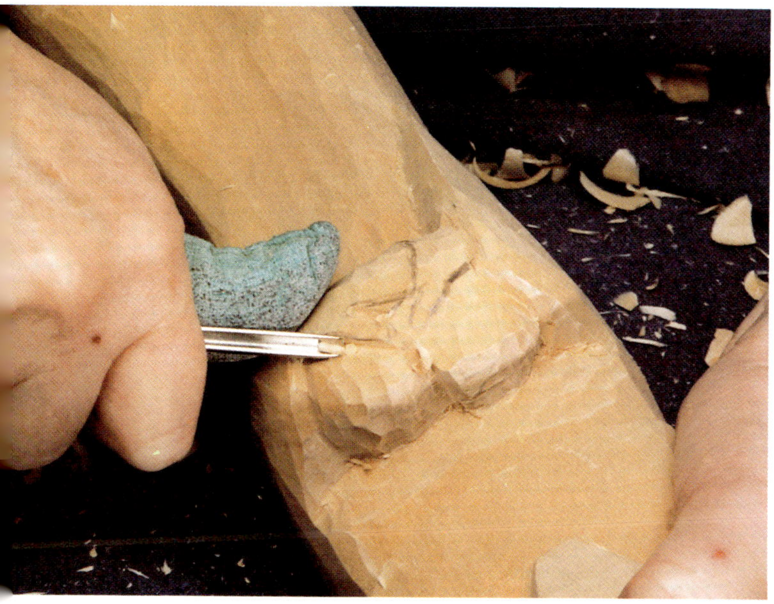

Use a deep veiner to go around the hands.

Do this all around the top hand.

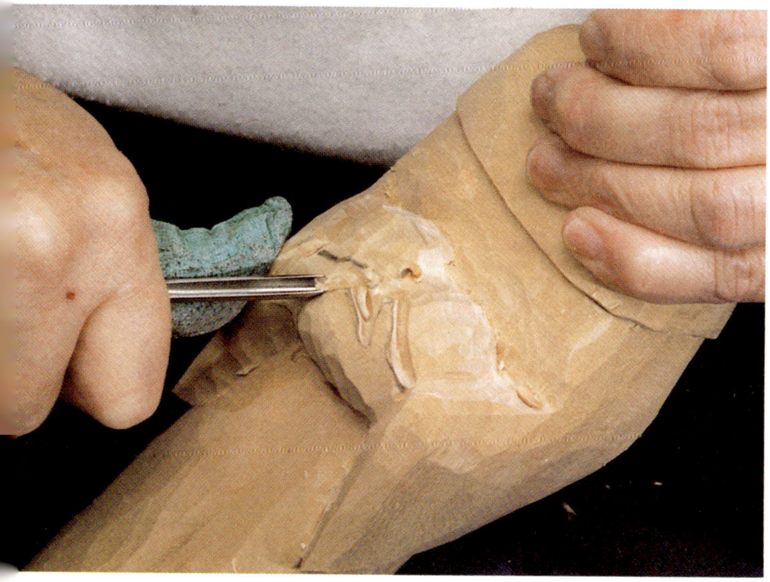

Do the top hand first. This will remove the lines of the lower hand, which will need to be redrawn.

Use a knife to take a little off the lower edge of the hand.

With a gouge or knife cut in to thin the wrist.

Again, go around the outline with a deep veiner.

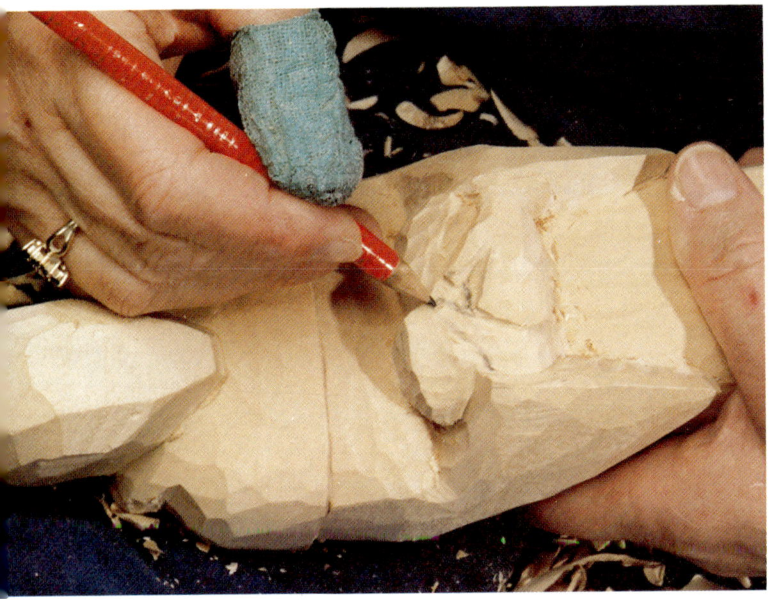

Redraw the lower hand. Basically all you will see is the thumb, the top edge of the forefinger...

Clean up and blend the lines with a knife.

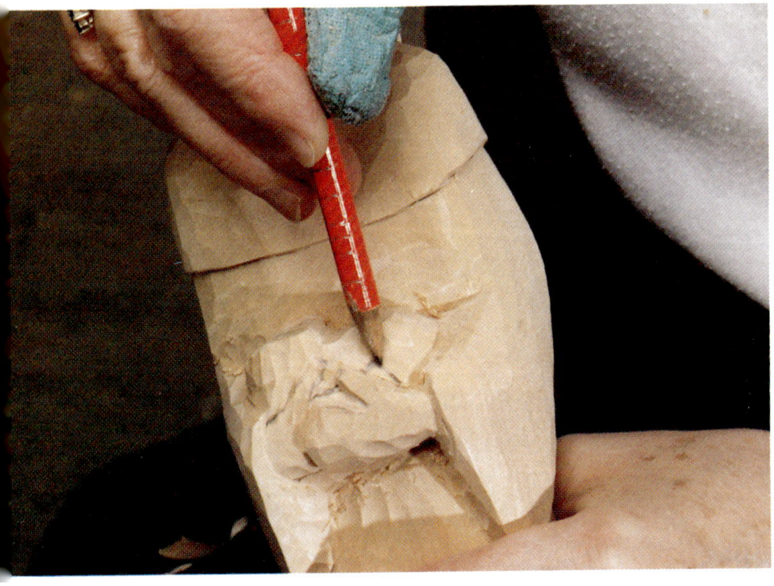

and a bit of the ends of the fingers.

Deepen under the wrist with a veiner.

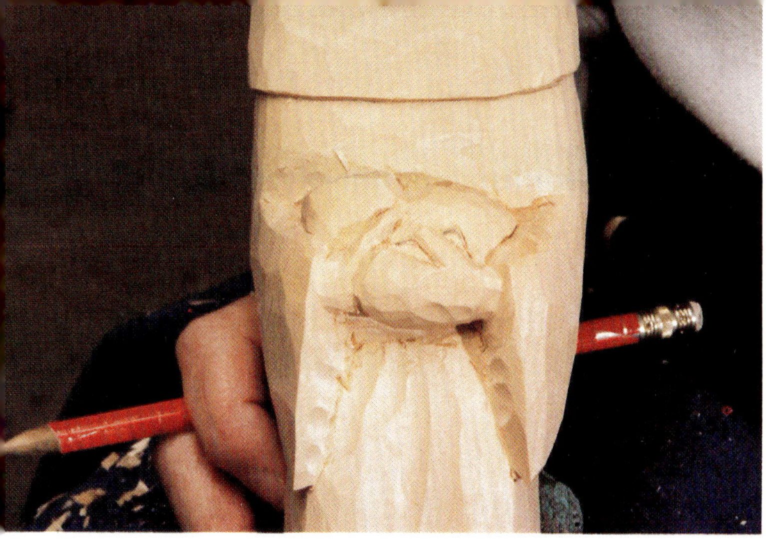

This should take you to this point. I leave the hands like this until the rabbit is carved.

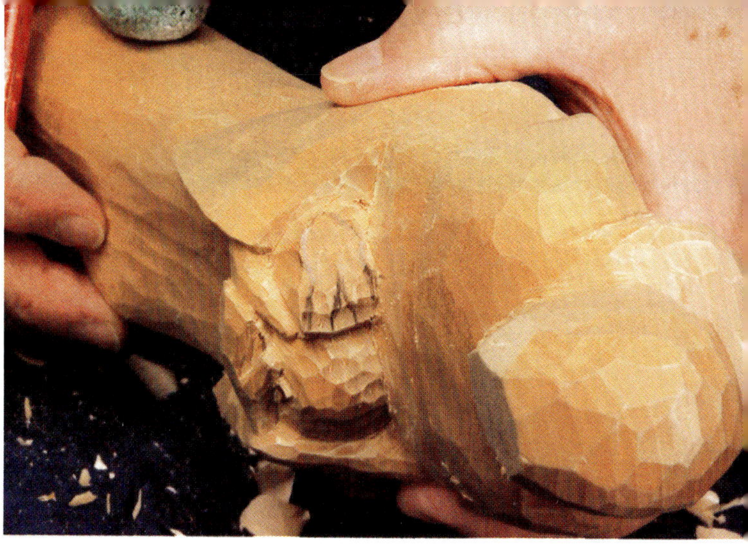

Draw in the top view of the head and ears.

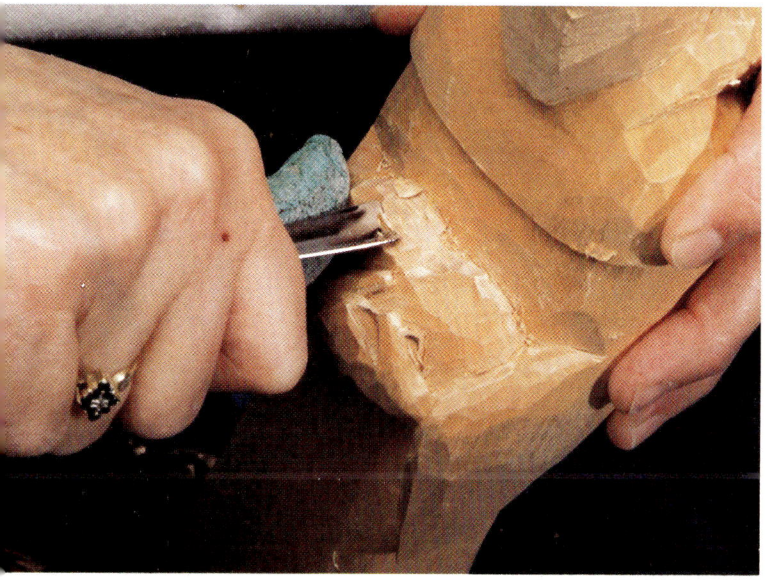

Use a gouge to lower the back of the ears.

Use a gouge to bring the head out from the body.

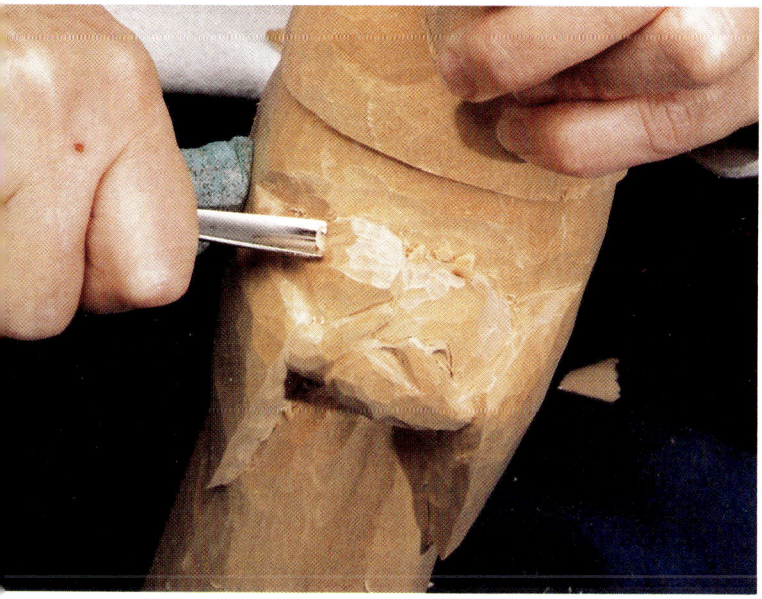

Take some off the end of the nose.

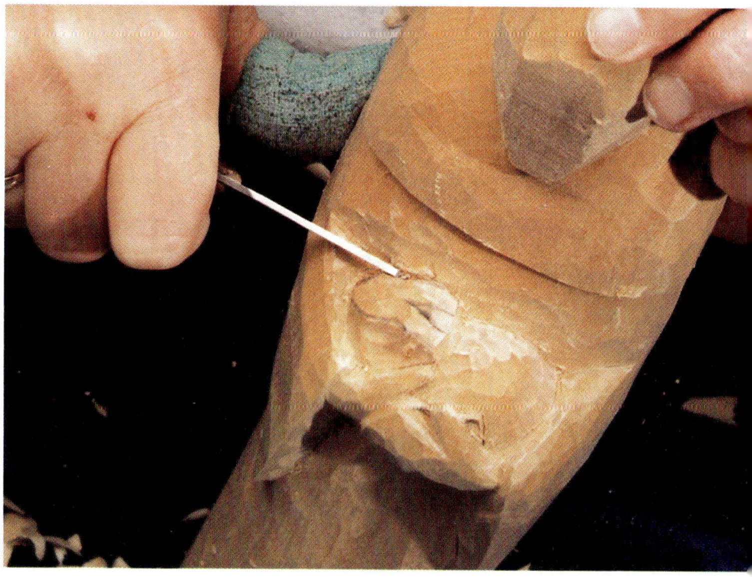

Cut a stop between the body and the front part of the ear and back of the head.

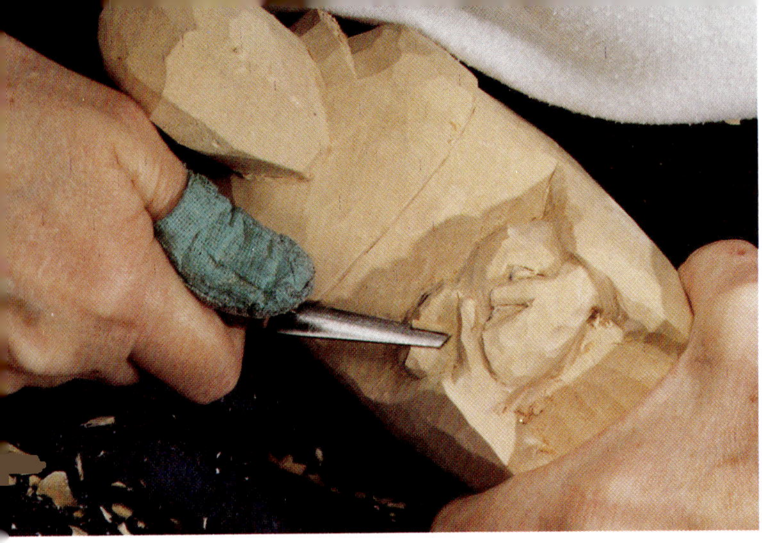

Shape the head down to the profile.

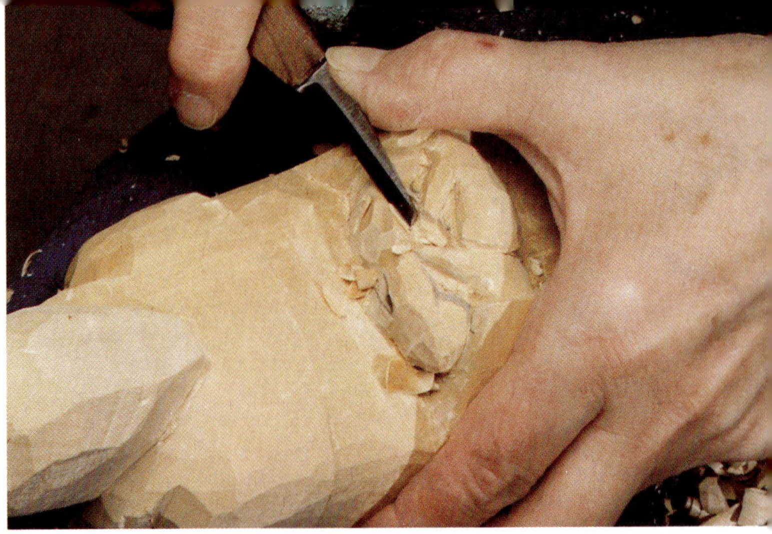

Round off the back of the rabbit.

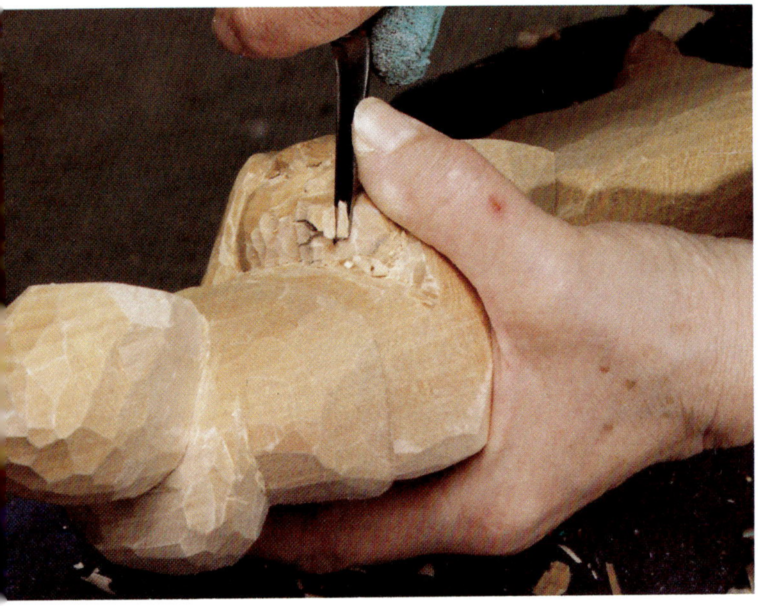

Use a curl cut to create a depression at the back of the head and the front of the ears on top.

Cut a stop under the jaw...

Draw in the lower edge of the ear and the bottom of the jaw.

and under the ear.

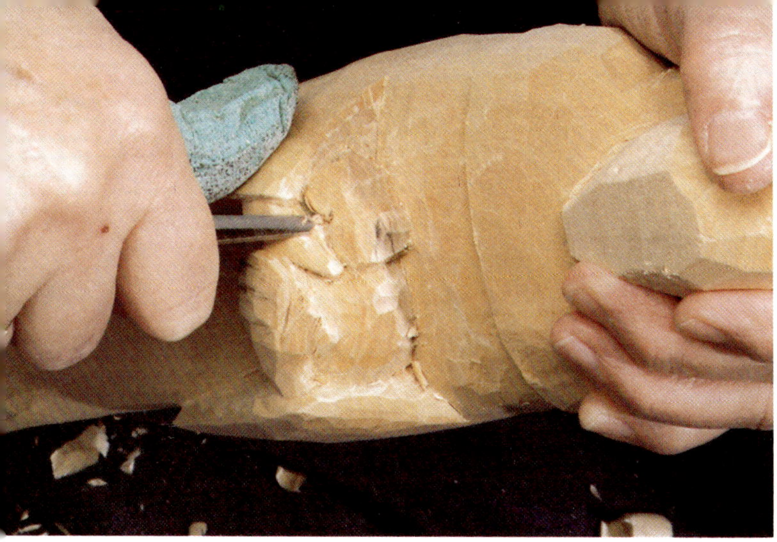

From the hand cut back under the ear the jaw.

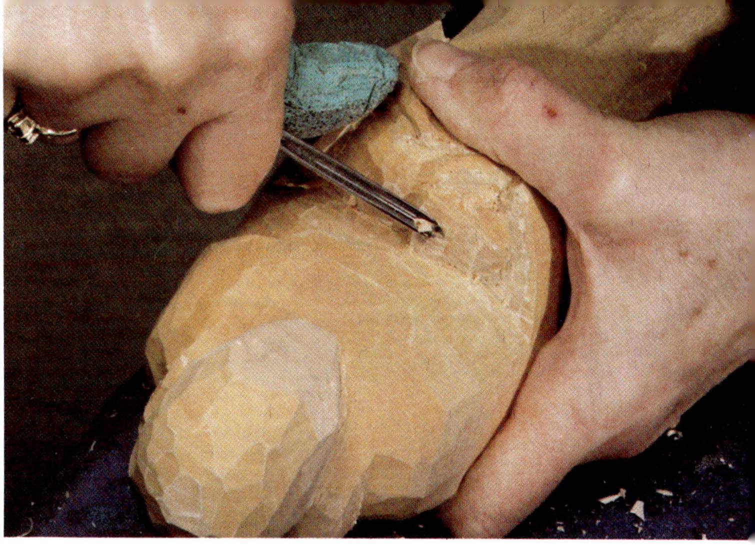

Use a veiner to clean out between the ears.

Clean the area out with a small veiner.

Use a knife to shape the ears.

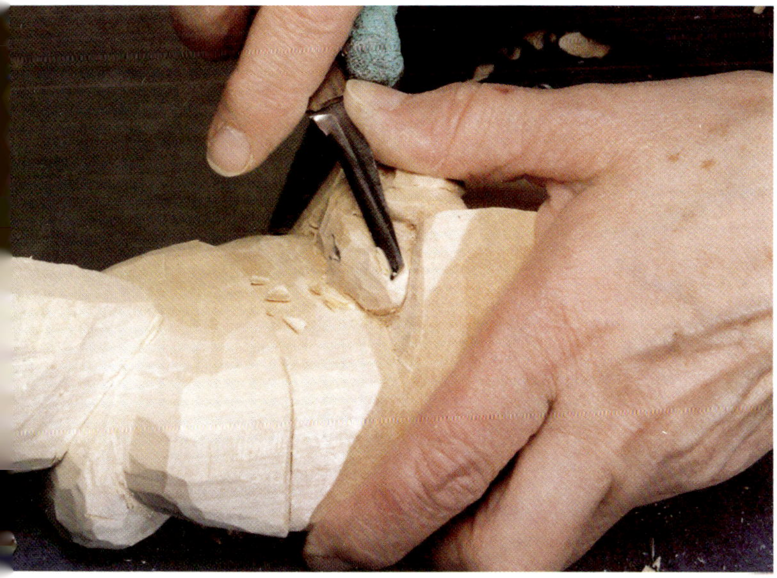

At the side of the head make a curl cut to create a place for the eye.

With a gouge cup the front of the ears.

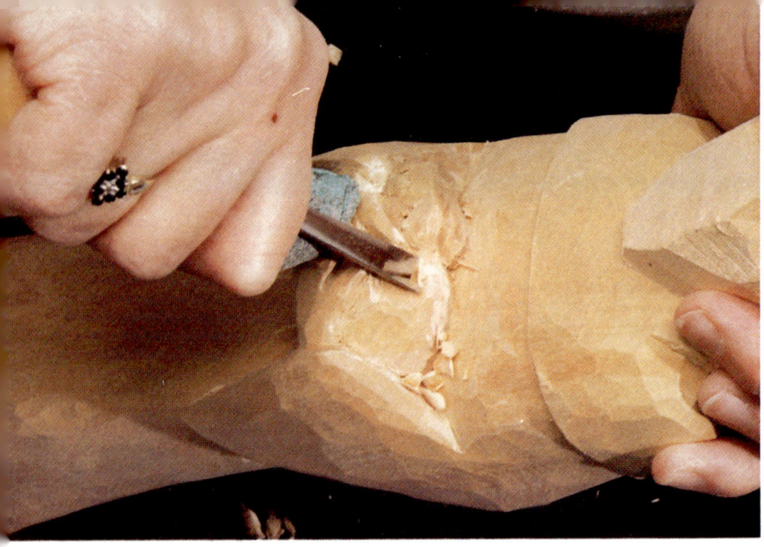

Move to the rabbit's body and trim it down using gouges.

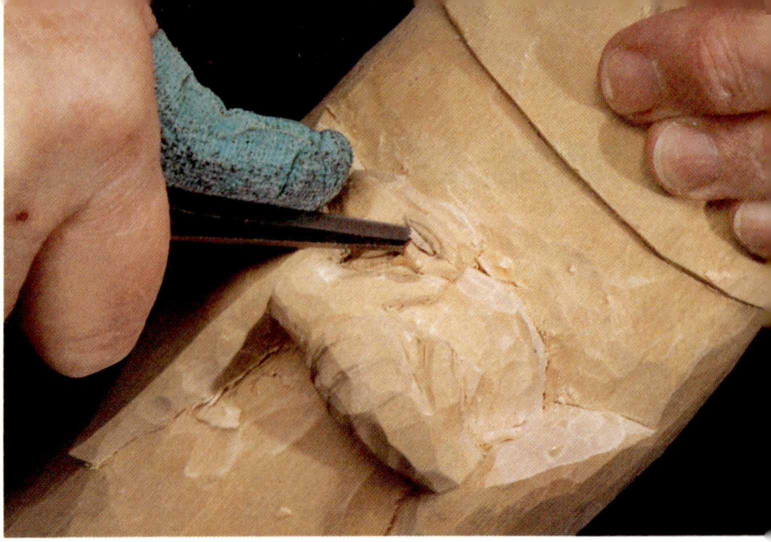

Slice back to it from the bottom.

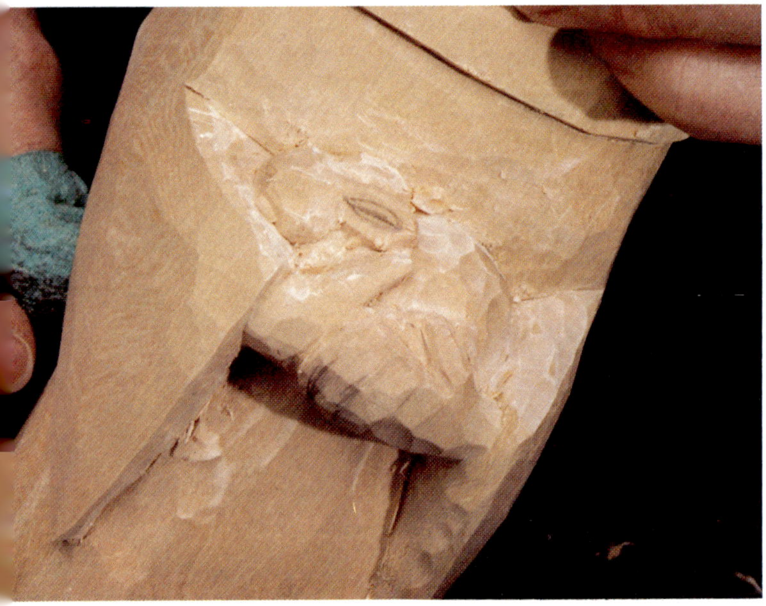

Draw the inside of the ear.

Turn the piece and slice back to it from the top.

Cut a stop down the center.

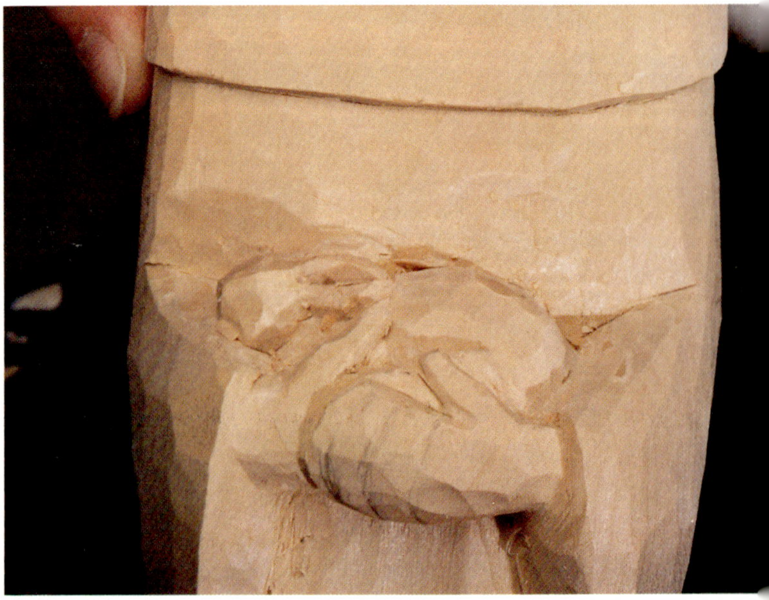

With a little cleaning you should end up with this result.

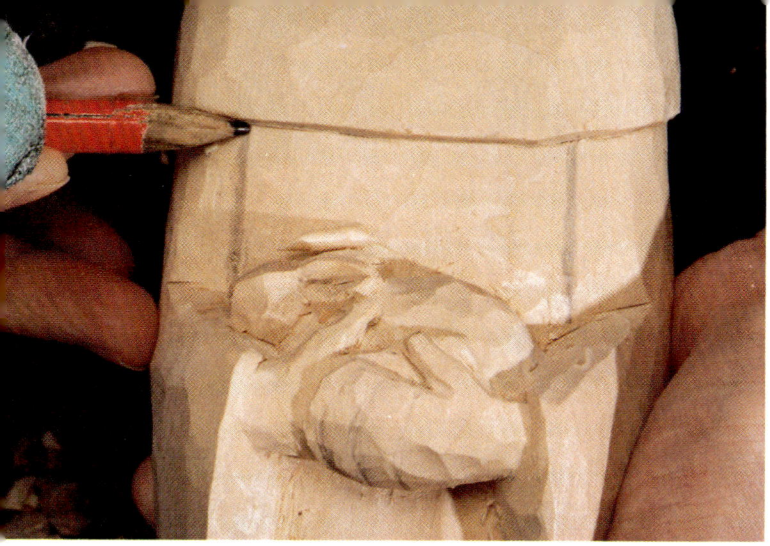

Draw in the inside of the arms.

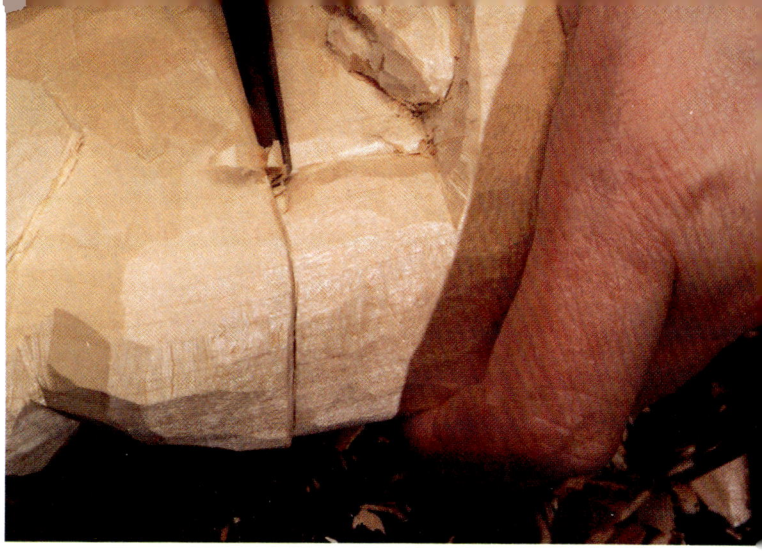

Do the same on the chest.

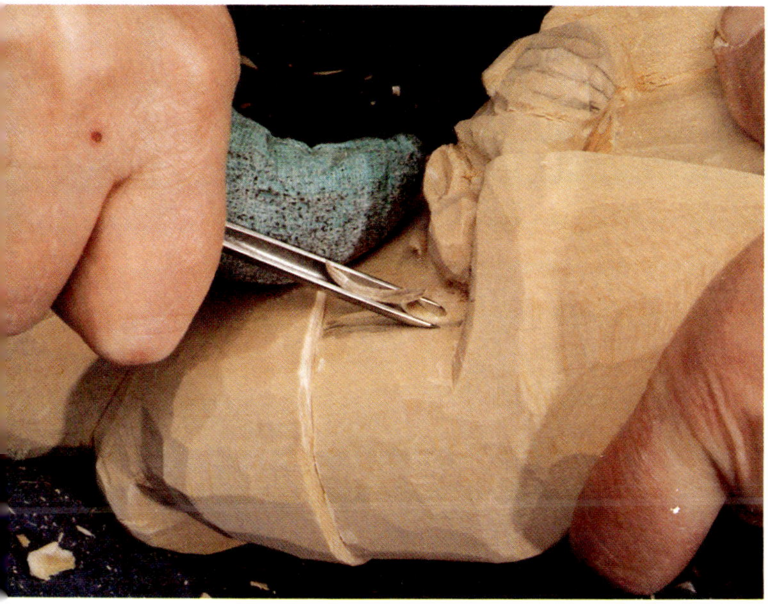

Go over the lines with a veiner.

Use the knife to deepen the crook of the elbow, giving the piece more depth.

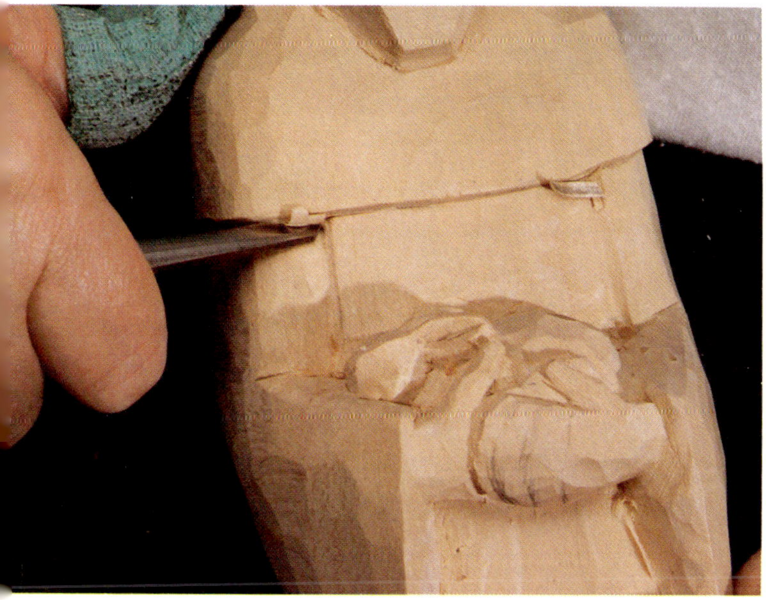

Round the arm with a knife.

Clean up the area with a skew.

Cut folds in the elbow by first cutting one way...

then the other.

then the other.

The result.

Repeat to create smaller folds. First one way...

On the top hand, draw the three lines of the knuckles.

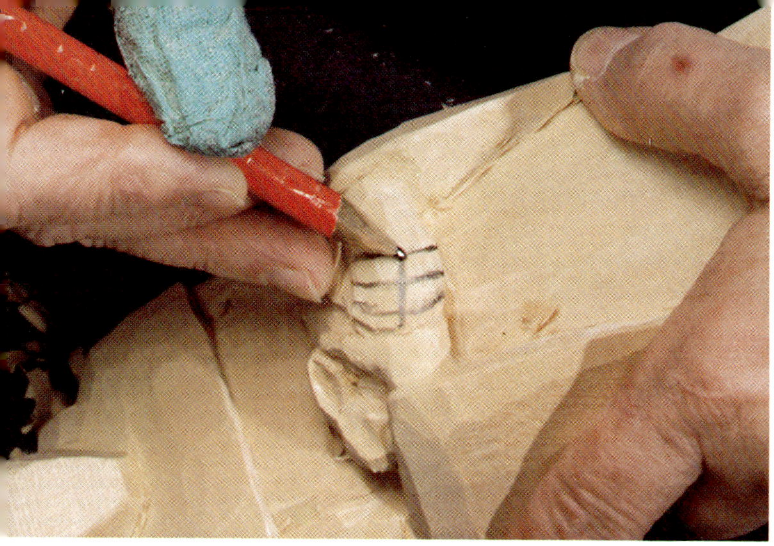

Mark the center line of the fingers first...

The result.

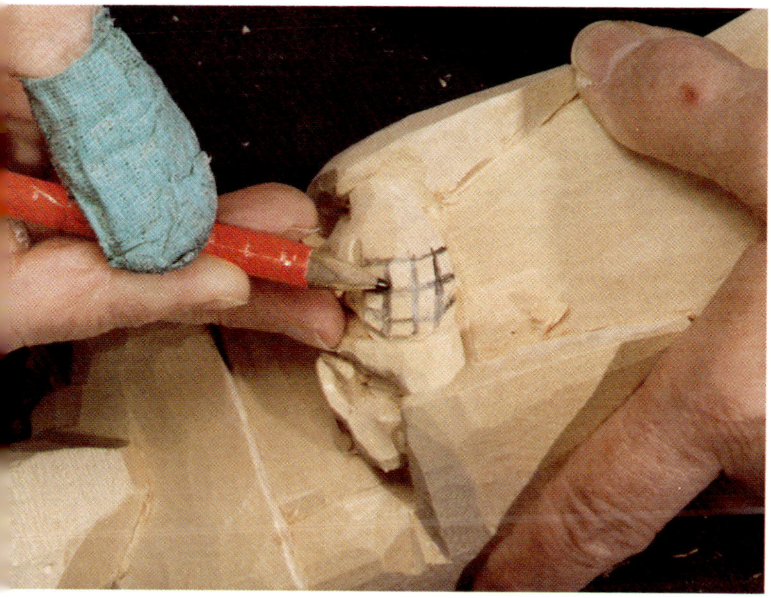

then the other two.

A knife slims the fingers and deepens the space between them. First cut one way then the other.

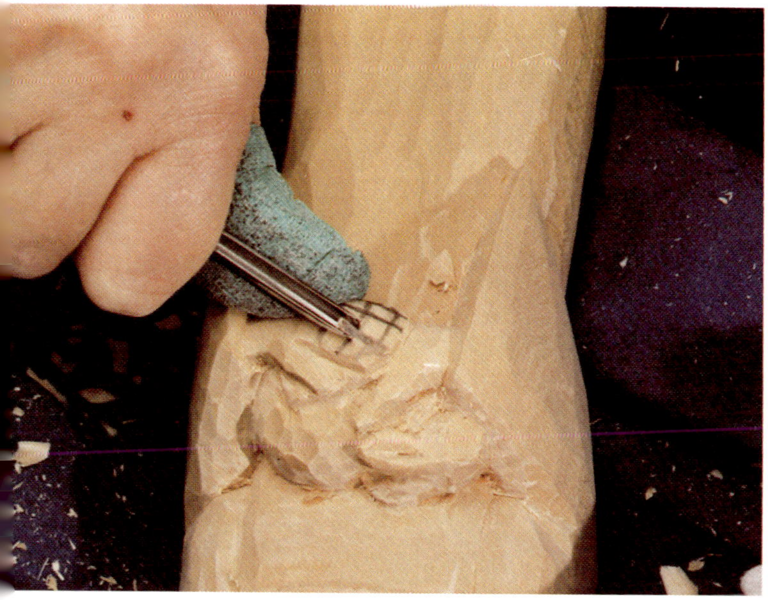

Follow the lines of the fingers with a veiner.

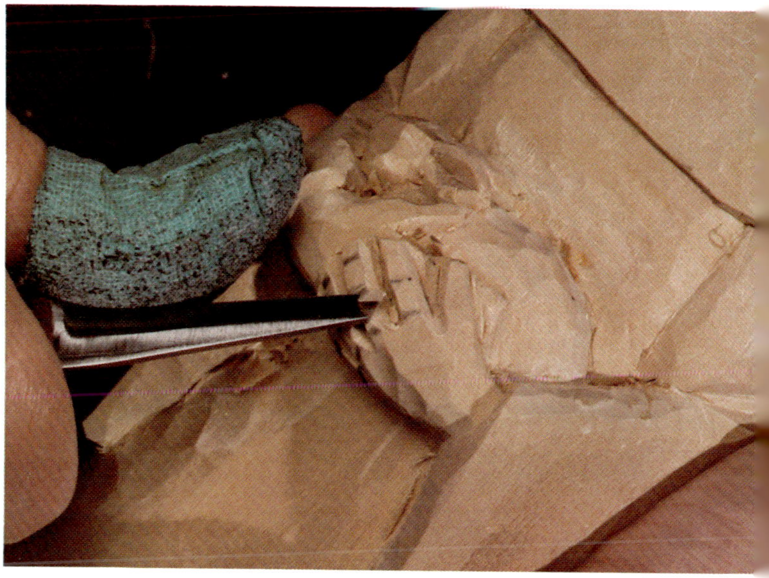

Working from knuckle to knuckle, take off the corners.

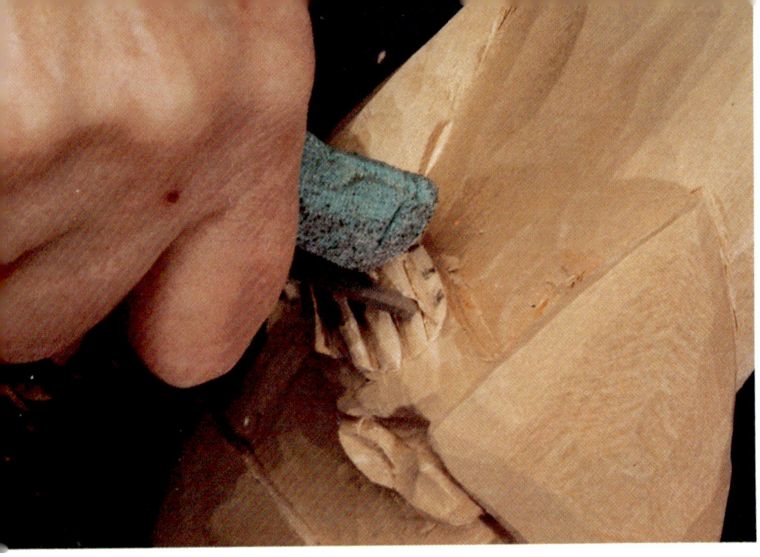

When the corners are off, go back and shape the finger, being careful not to cut off a knuckle.

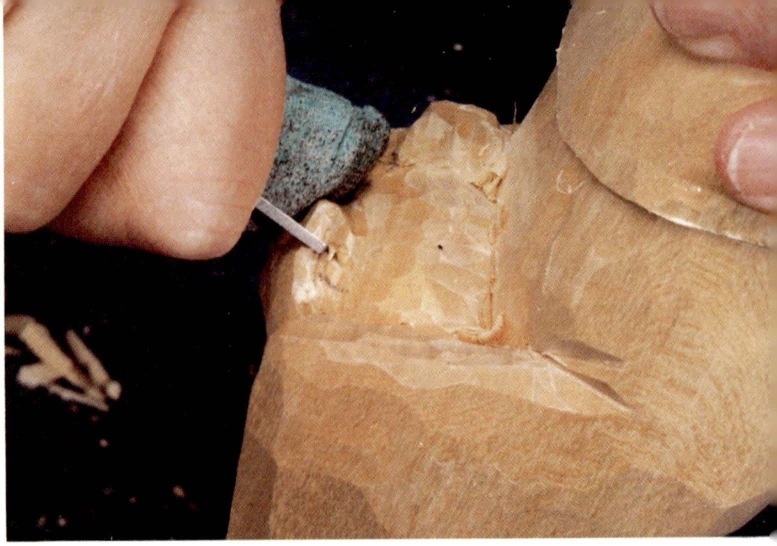

Use the knife to carve the lines.

Go back and round off the ends of the fingers.

It's a little tough in here. Get a sharp point on your knife, and be careful not to cut off the thumb.

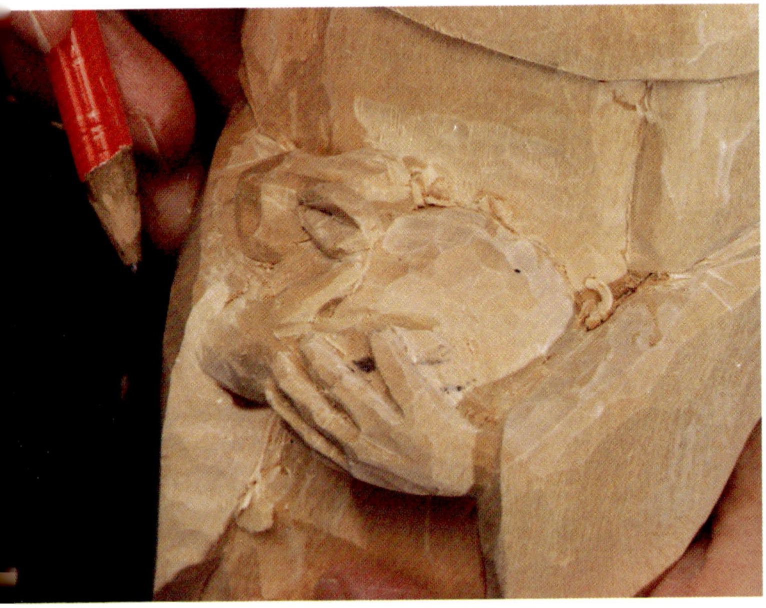

Draw in the lines of the fingers of the bottom hand.

Draw in a few folds on the sleeves.

With a knife make shallow curls cuts along the folds.

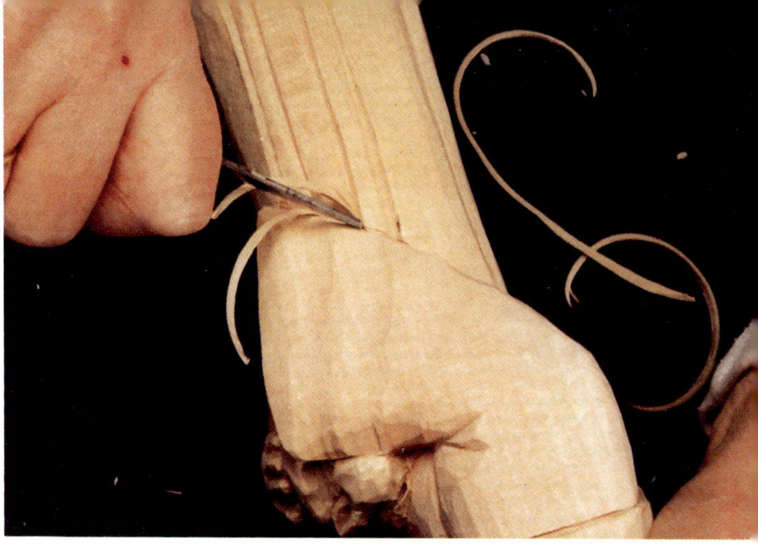

Cut the curls off beneath the arm.

Draw the ends of the cincture as it hangs.

Remove wood from the robe with a skew to bring it down to the level of the belt.

Go around the outline of the belt with a small V-tool.

Go back and clean up the lines with the V-tool.

Draw three knots in the back portion of belt. These stand for the holy trinity.

The edges of the belt should taper in a bit as they go into the knot.

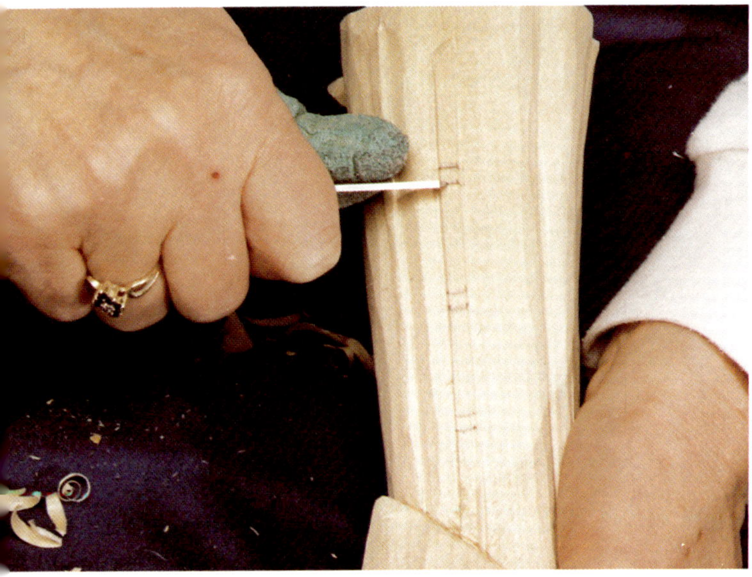

Cut a shallow stop in each line of the knot...

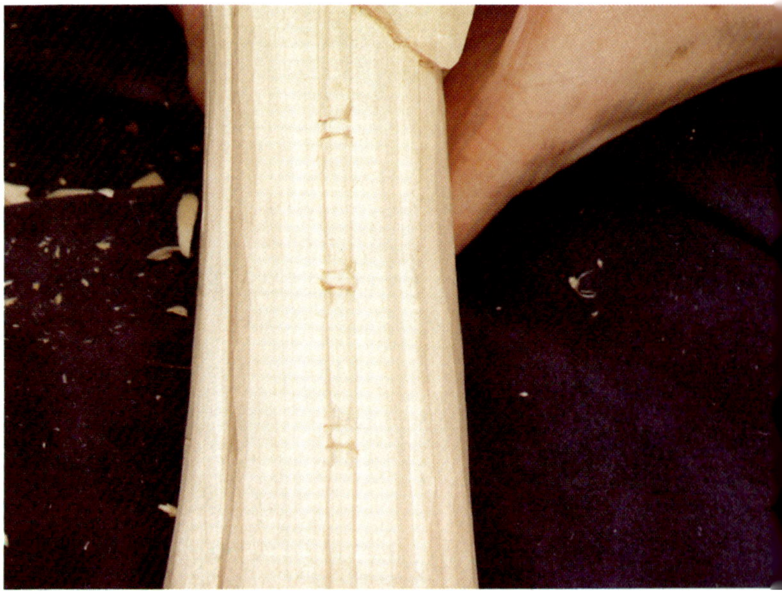

Rounding the belt some gives this result.

and cut back to it from the belt.

Round the front part of the belt.

Draw in the spiral of the rope belt. Leave room at the ends for tassels.

At the acute end of the cuts, push the tip of your knife in perpendicular to the spirals. This give the rope a realistic look.

Cut shallow angled stop cuts in the lines one way.

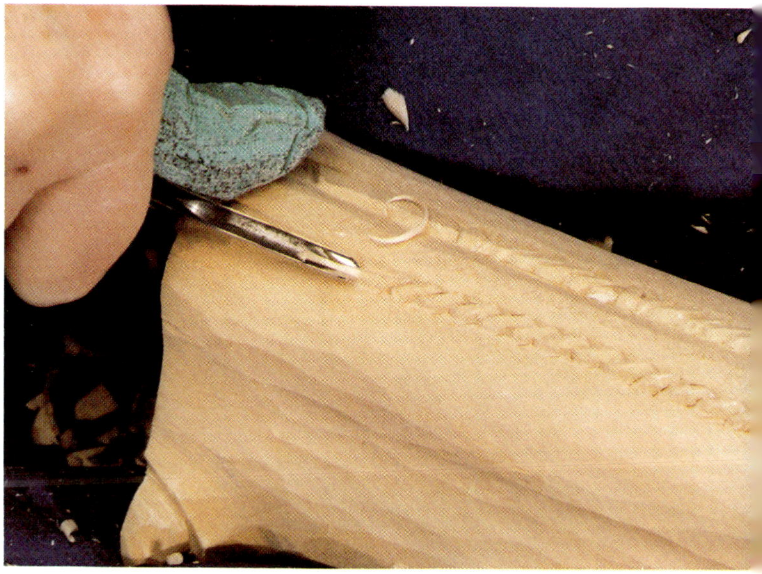

Add detail to the tassels with a veiner.

Then turn the piece and cut the other way, popping out the slices.

The result.

Draw the sole of the sandal...

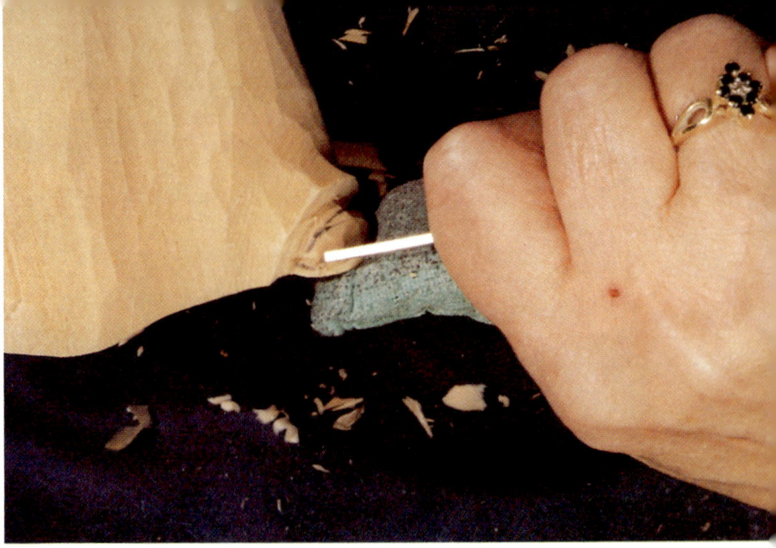

and cut back to it from the foot.

and the strap.

Cut a stop in the line of the strap...

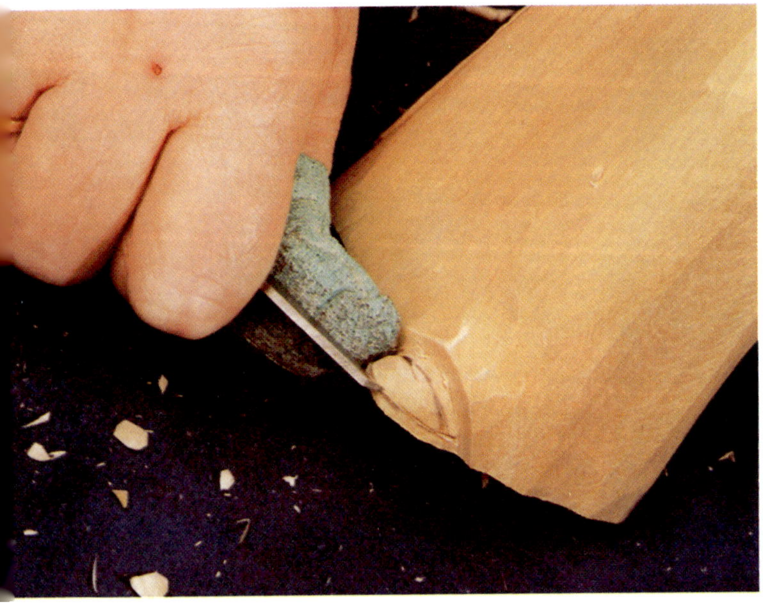

Cut a stop in the line of the sole...

and back to it from the foot.

Mark the toes.

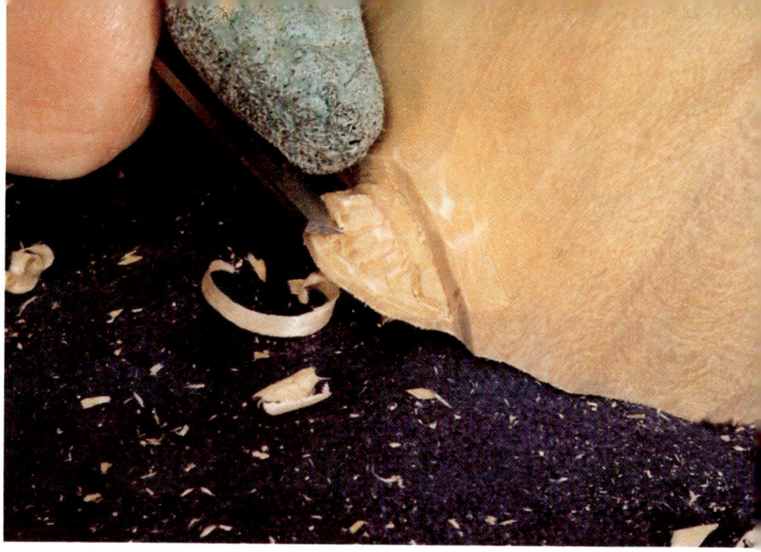

Take a sliver off the end of the toe for the toenail.

With a V-tool go between the toes.

Progress.

Round off between the toes.

Narrow and round the belt in the back.

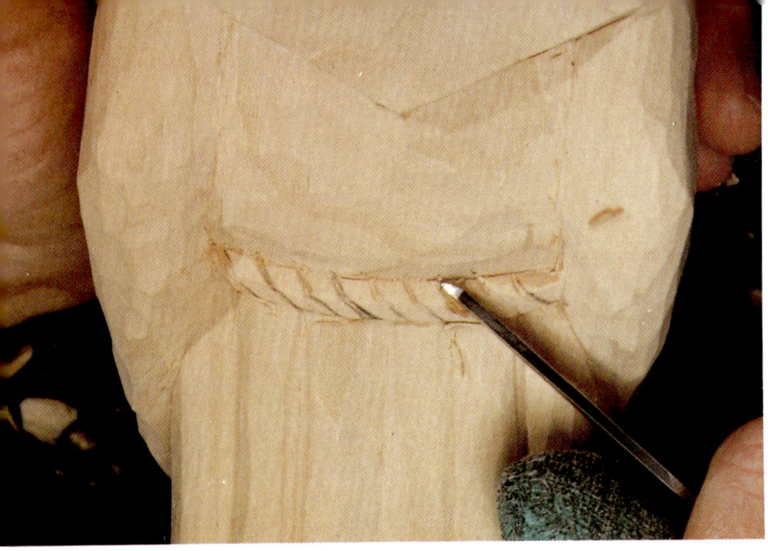
Repeat the spiraling process along the back of the belt.

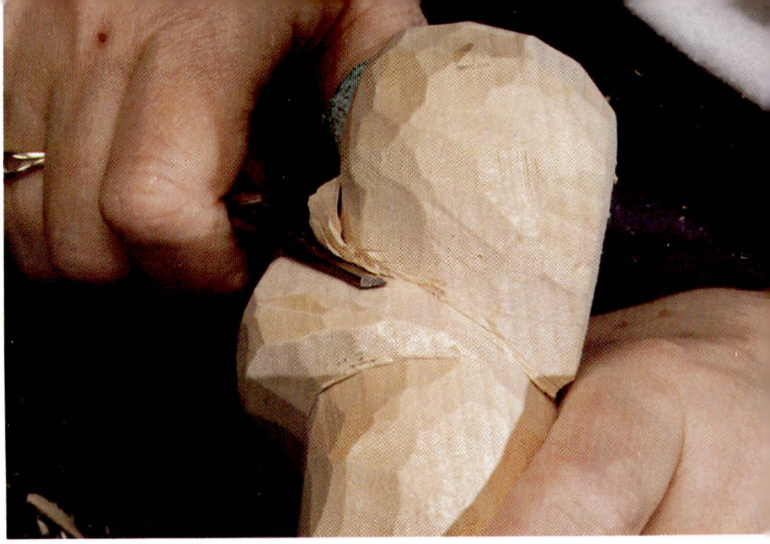
Begin work on the hood by trimming it down a bit. It is too heavy.

Progress.

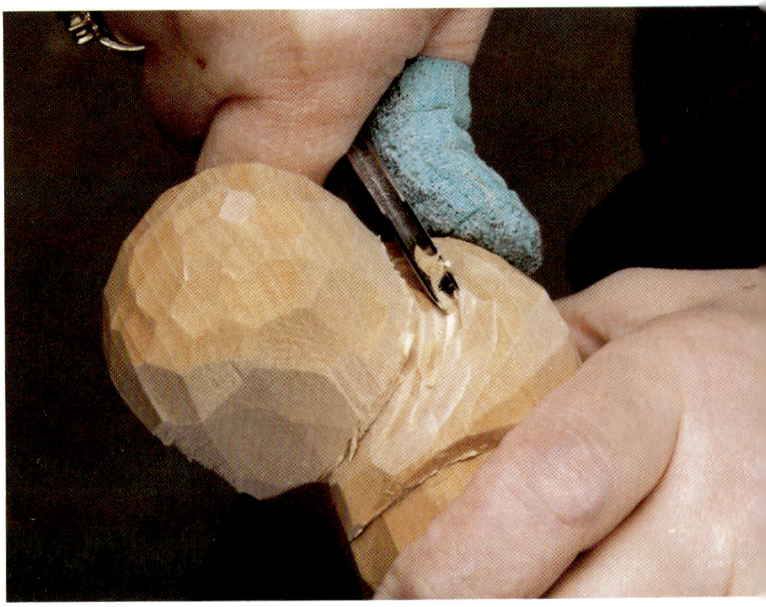
Use the gouge to give yourself a little working room.

Add some gathering wrinkles above the belt using a V-tool

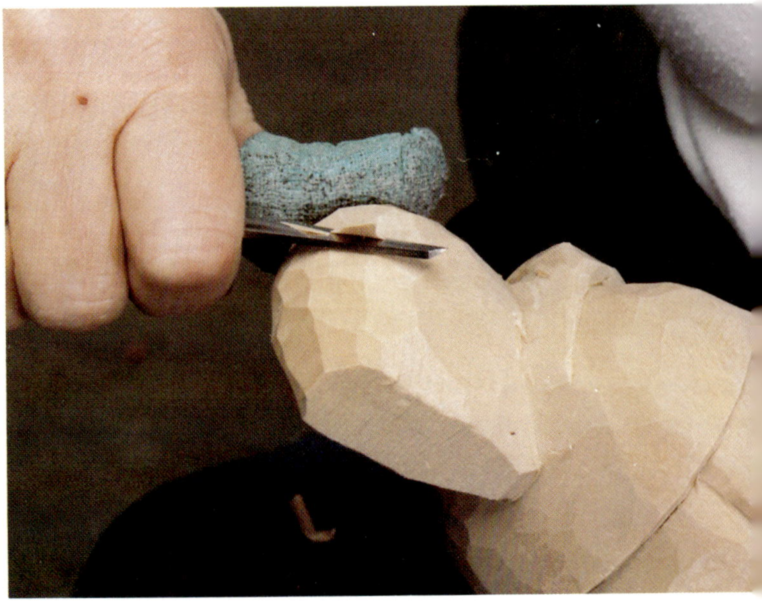
Trim the head to make it proportional to the body.

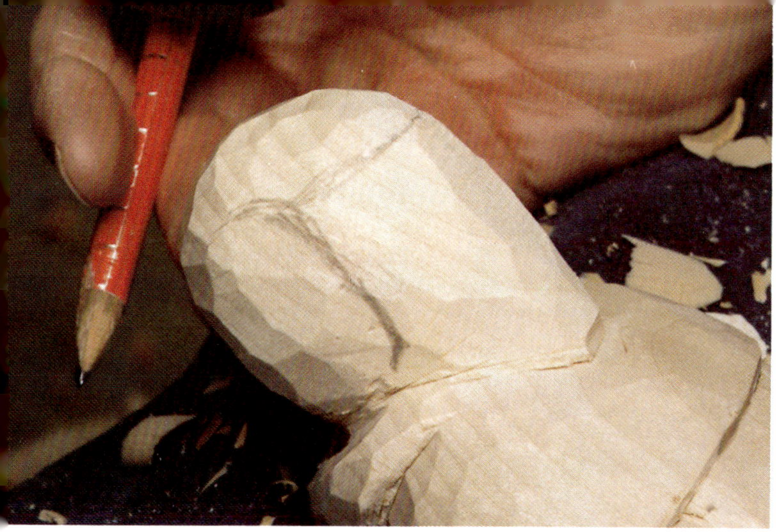

Draw in the hair line.

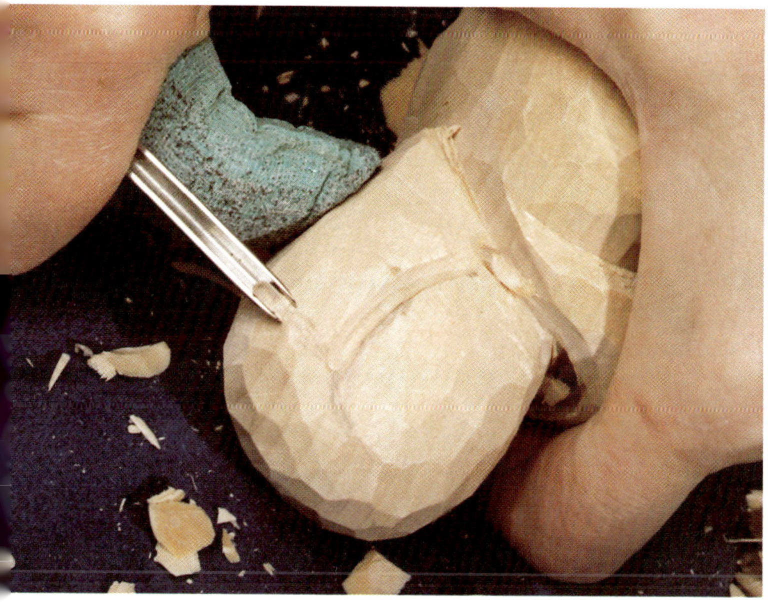

Follow the hair line with the deep veiner.

Thin the face back to the line.

Draw the line of the end of the nose and trim the upper face back to the hairline.

You are looking for this kind of slope.

Draw the center line and the sides of the nose.

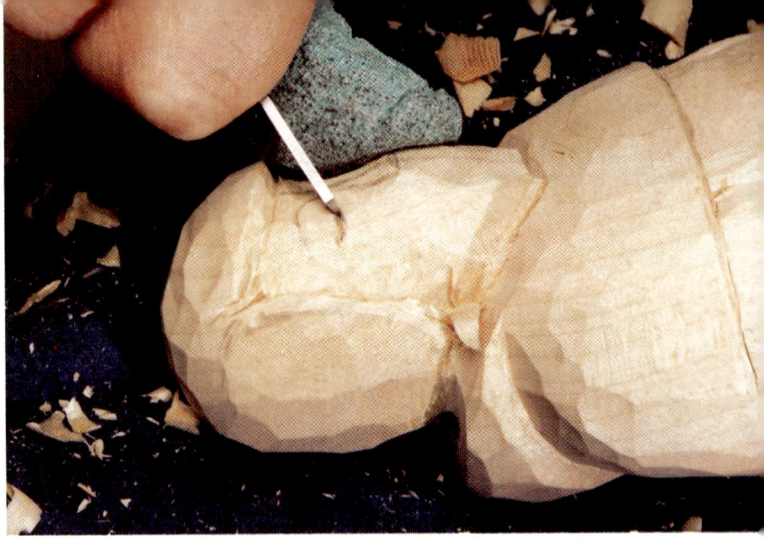

Cut stops in the lines of the eyes.

Continue the nose lines around to make the line of the eyebrows.

Cut from underneath to take out just a sliver of wood.

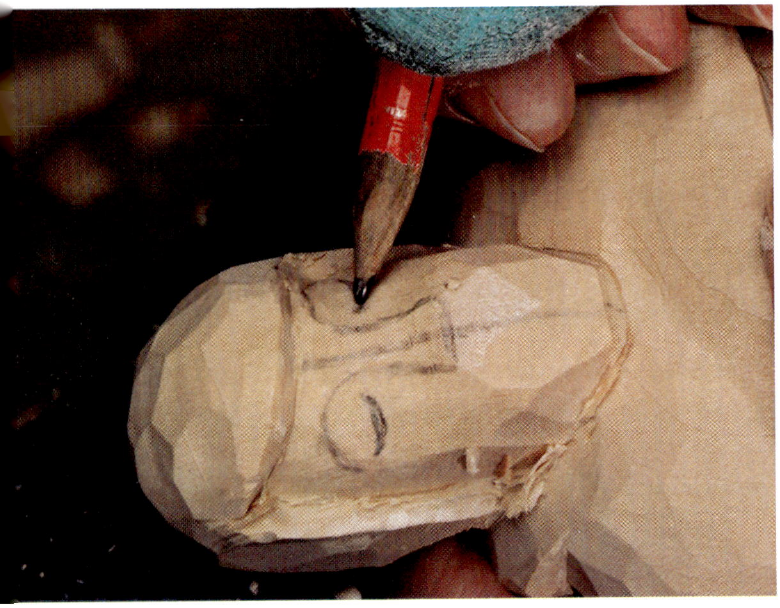

Draw the lines of the closed eyes.

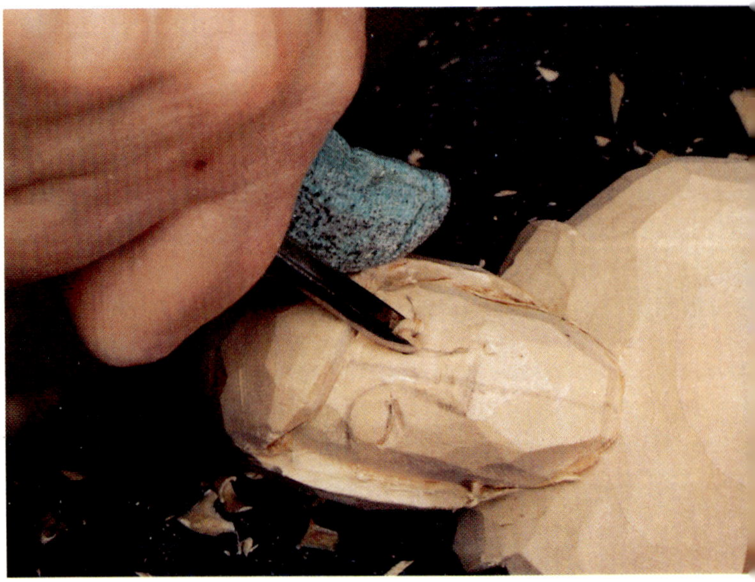

With a deep veiner start at the top of the eyebrow (about halfway) and follow the line of the nose.

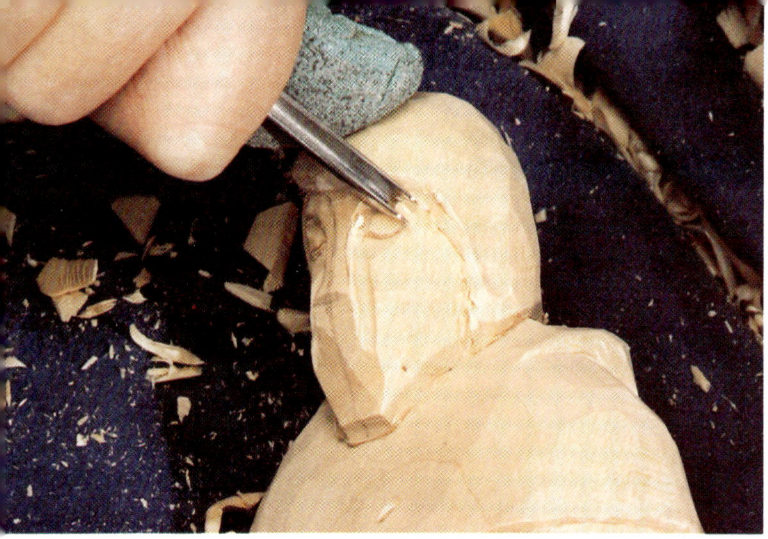

Then start at the same spot and follow the line out to the end of the eyebrow.

Several passes will create the rough shape of the cheek.

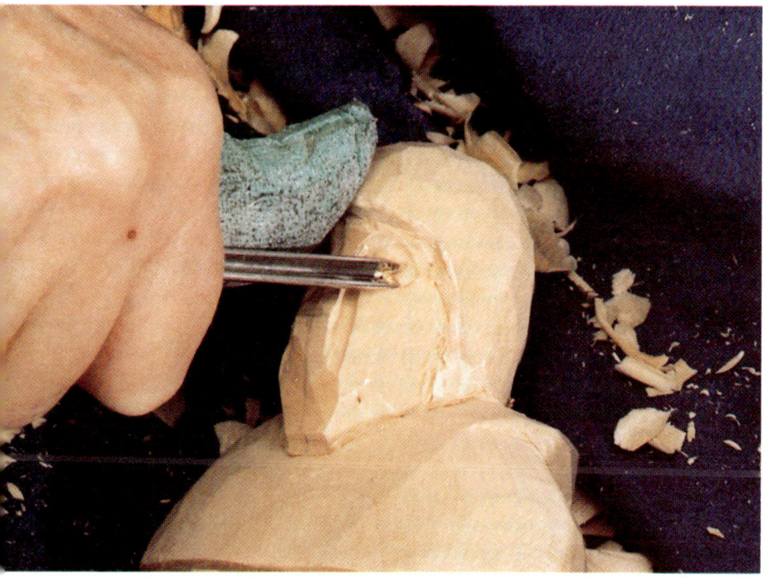

With the same veiner go beneath the line of the eye.

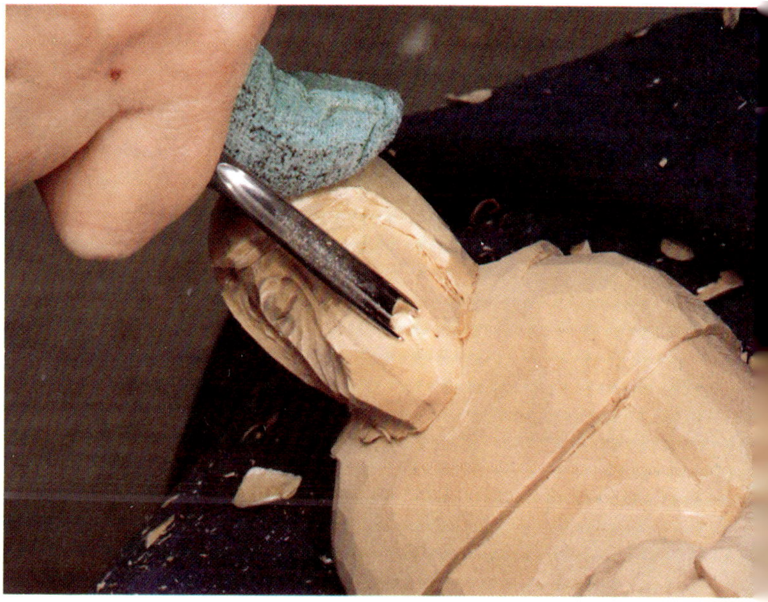

With a broader flatter gouge smooth up the area beside the nose.

Come down the side of the nose.

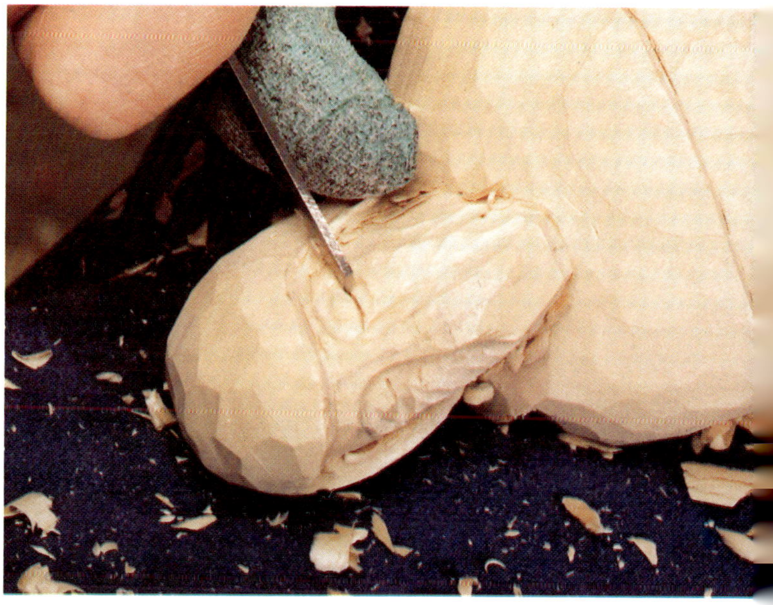

Go back and deepen the line of the eye, first with a stop cut...

then by cutting back to it from the cheek.

Cut the end of the nose with a angled stop...

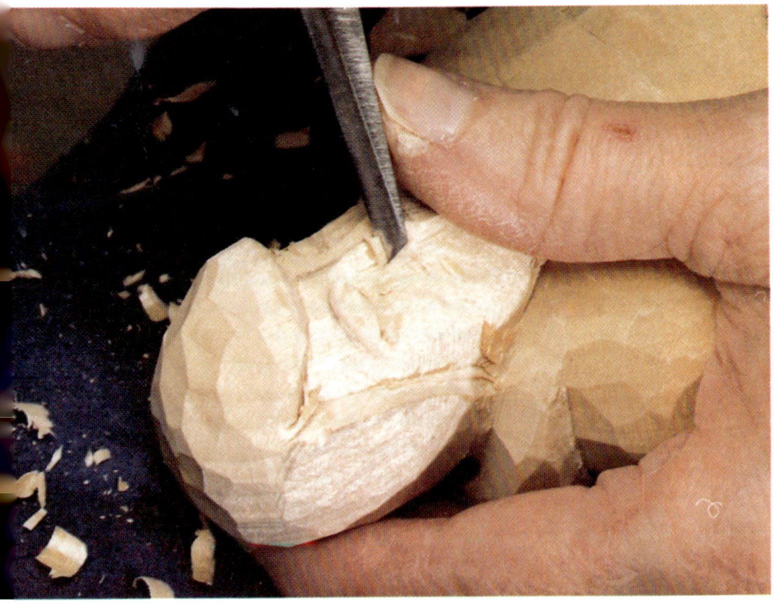

Shape the nose with the knife.

and a trim back from the lip.

Clean up the cheeks with the knife.

Deepen the cut by repeating, but don't flatten the upper lip.

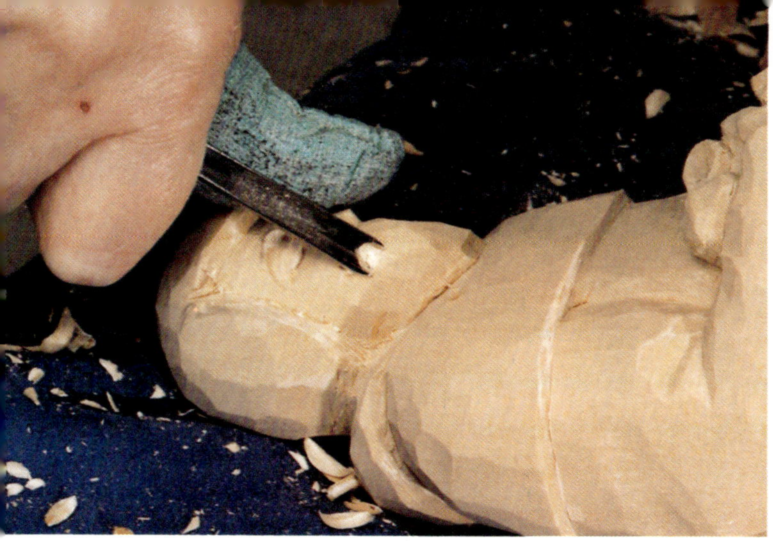

With a gouge follow the line of the cheek around the outside of the mouth.

Draw the hairline and the area for the ear.

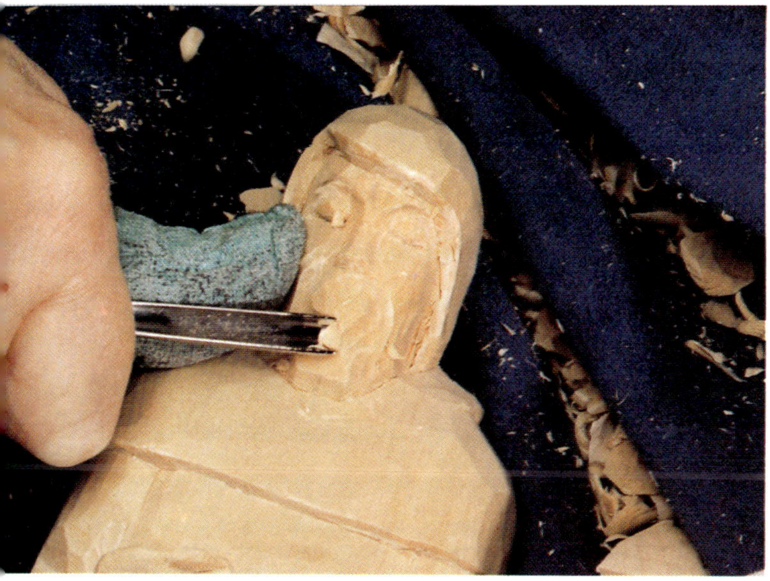

Continue around the mouth with the gouge, coming under the lip across the chin.

Make a v-cut along the hair line.

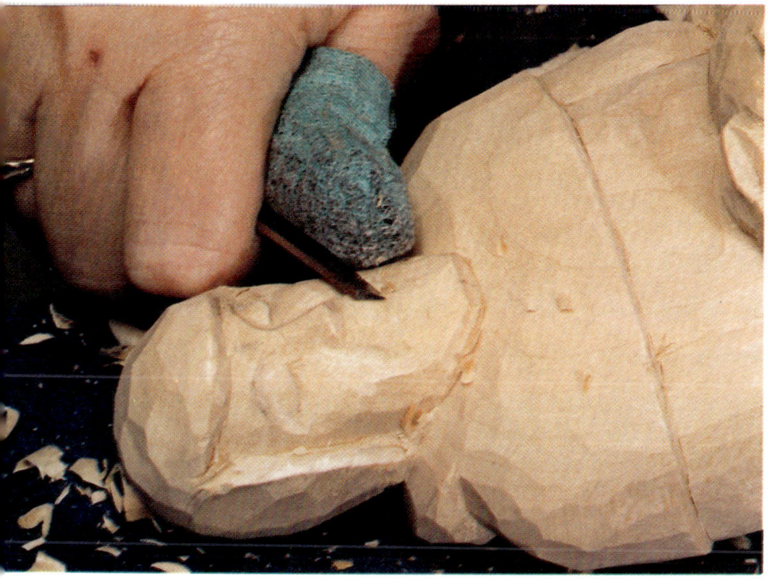

Smooth the mound for the mouth with the knife.

Redraw the ear area.

Cut a stop around the ear.

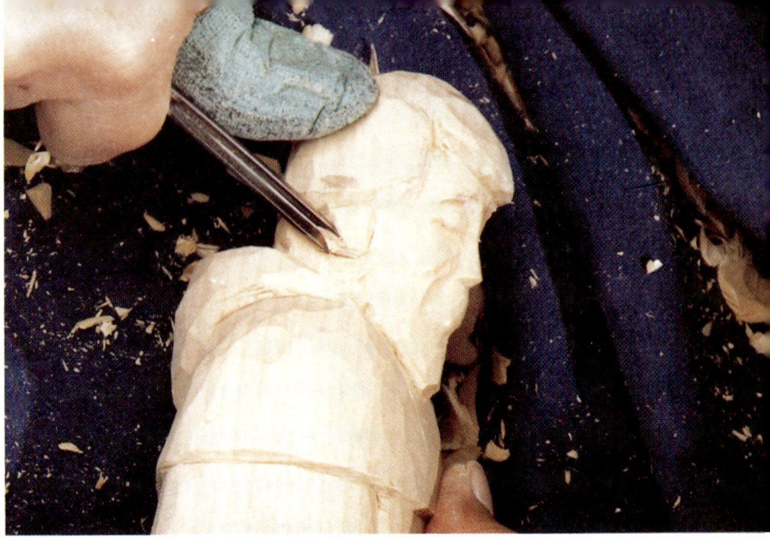

and use a gouge to remove the excess.

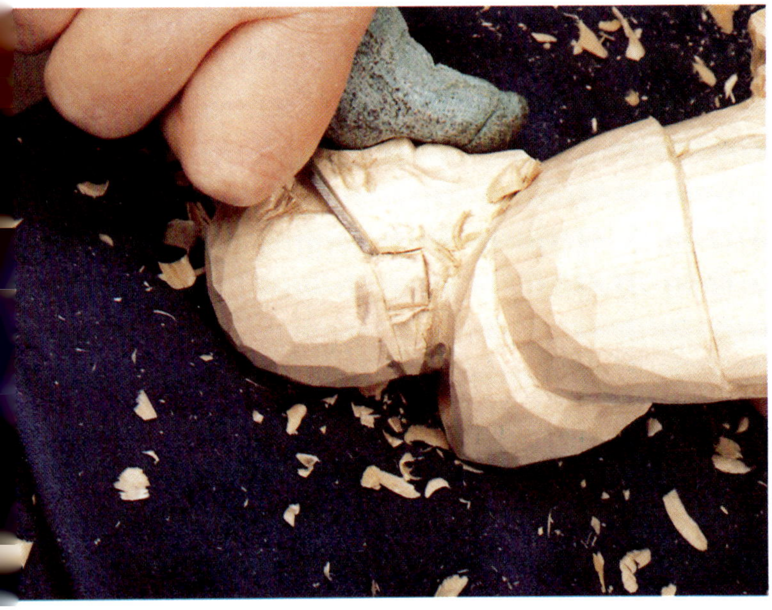

Trim back to it from the face and neck.

Use a curl cut to cup the inside of the ear.

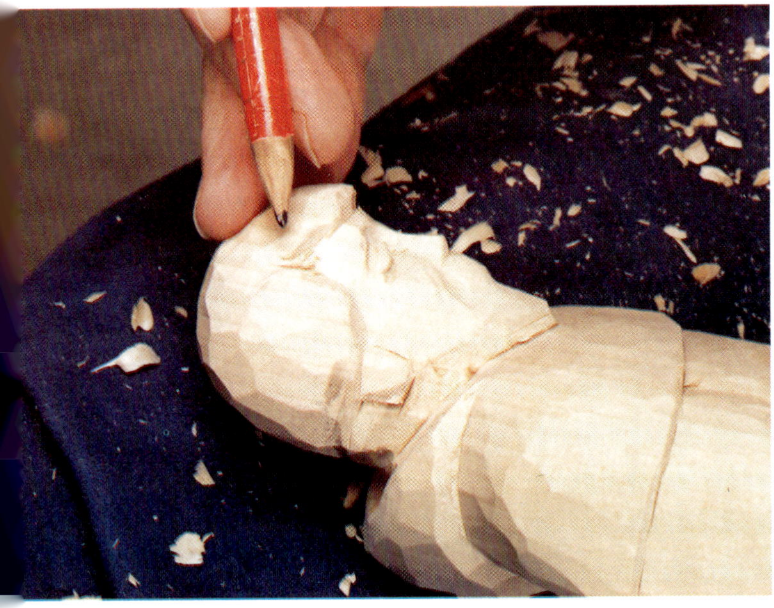

Draw the shape of the back of the ear...

Continue to define the hair line.

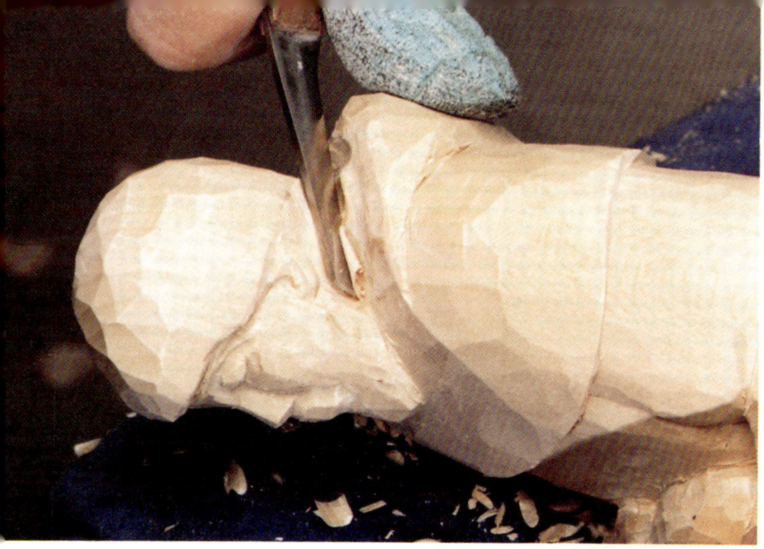

Form the jaw/beard line under the ear.

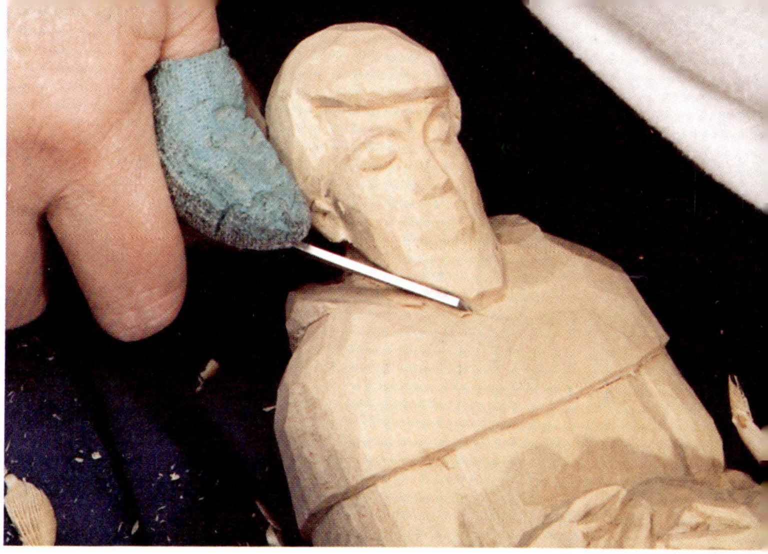

And back down the line of the beard.

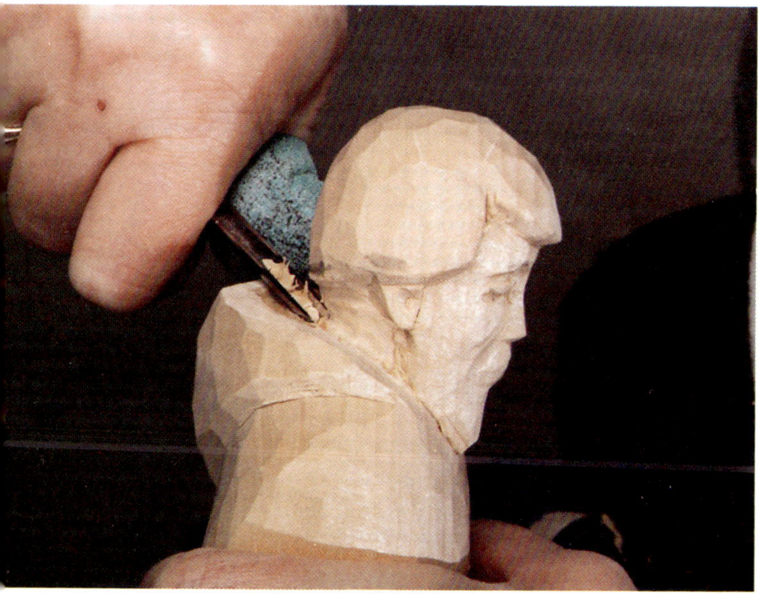

A gouge slims the back of the neck and creates a collar line.

Draw the line of the mouth...

Undercut the beard by coming across the chest...

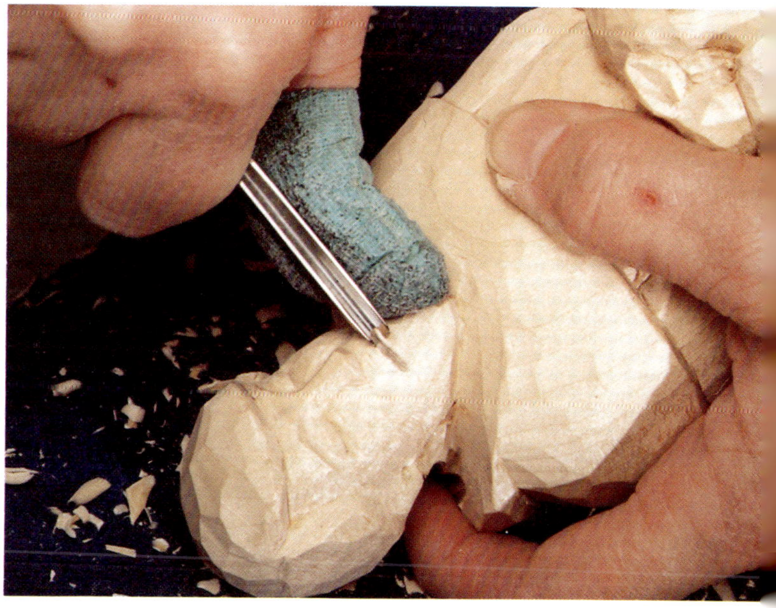

and go over it with a veiner.

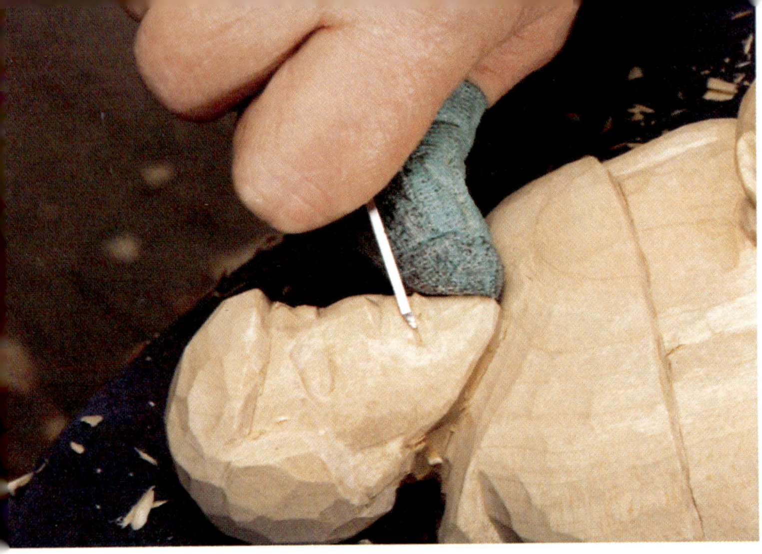

Take a knife and lightly shape the upper lip...

At the corners of the bottom lip, cut in to bring it under the upper.

and the lower lip.

Mark the angel's fingerprint under the nose...

Reduce the area between the nose and the lip.

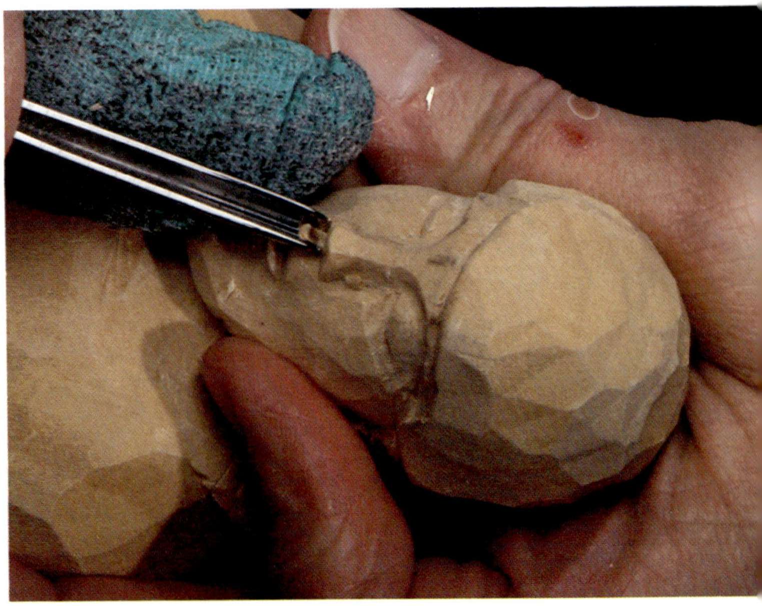

follow it with a veiner...

and nip it off with a knife.

Cut a stop in it.

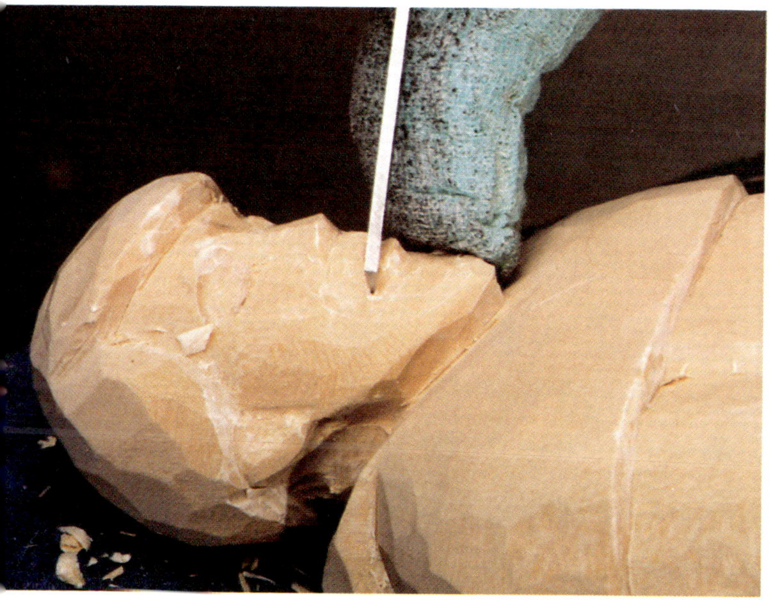

Press the end of the knife  into the corner of the mouth to make it look deeper.

Trim back to it from the mantle.

Draw the line of the hood.

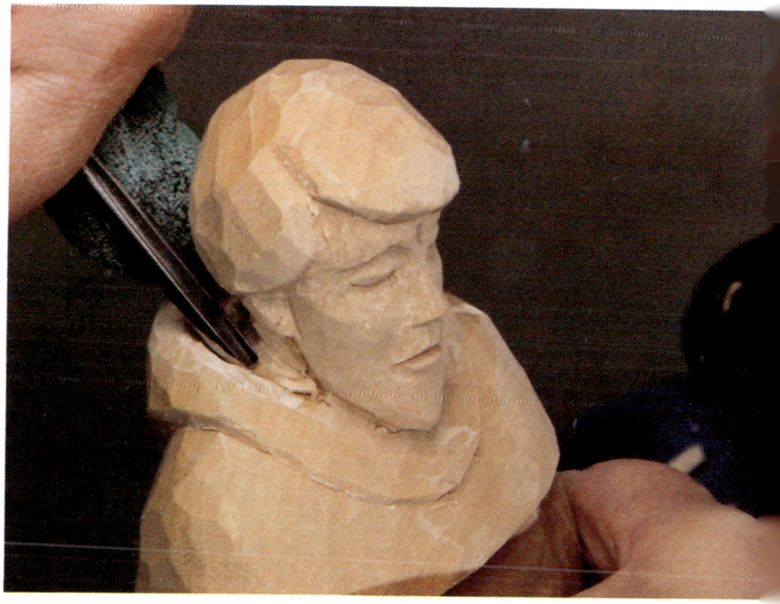

Use a deep veiner to carry the opening of the robe under the beard.

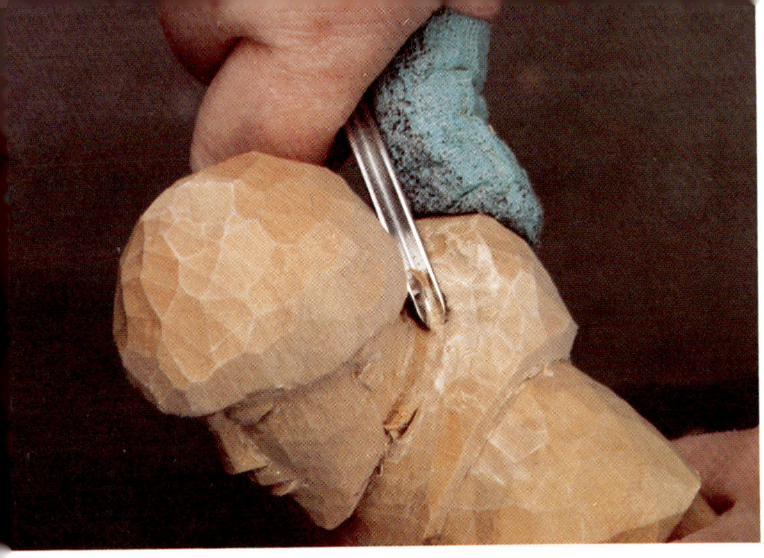

Continue that opening around the back as well.

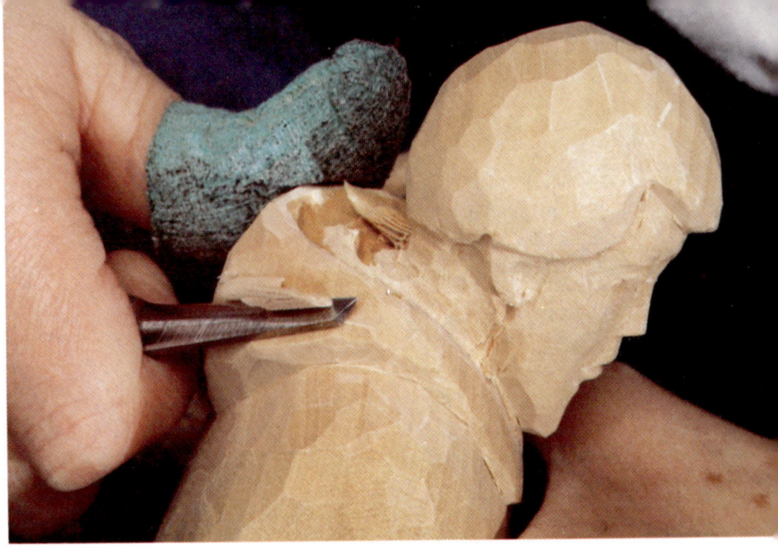

Use a curl cut to create a wrinkle or two in the hood.

Smooth and shape the hood with a knife.

Mark the head where hair will be removed.

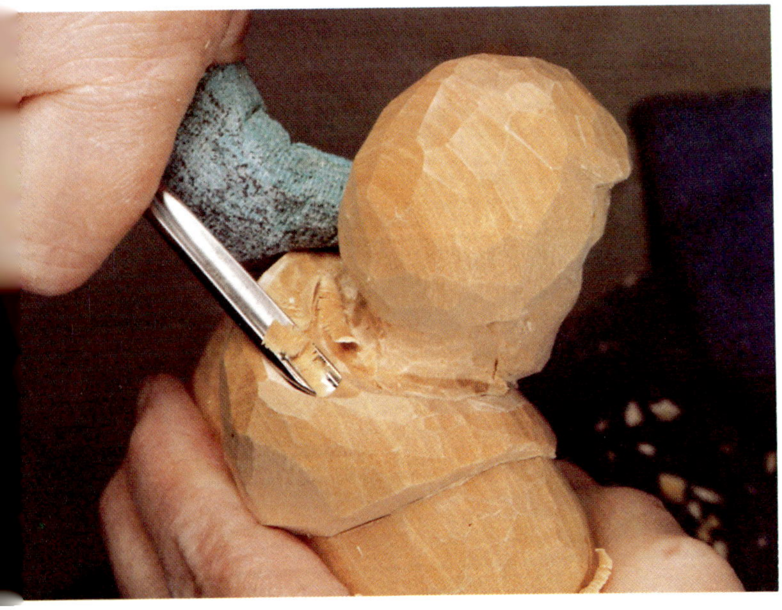

Open up the inside of the hood with a gouge.

Begin from the hair and work toward the crown to remove the hair.

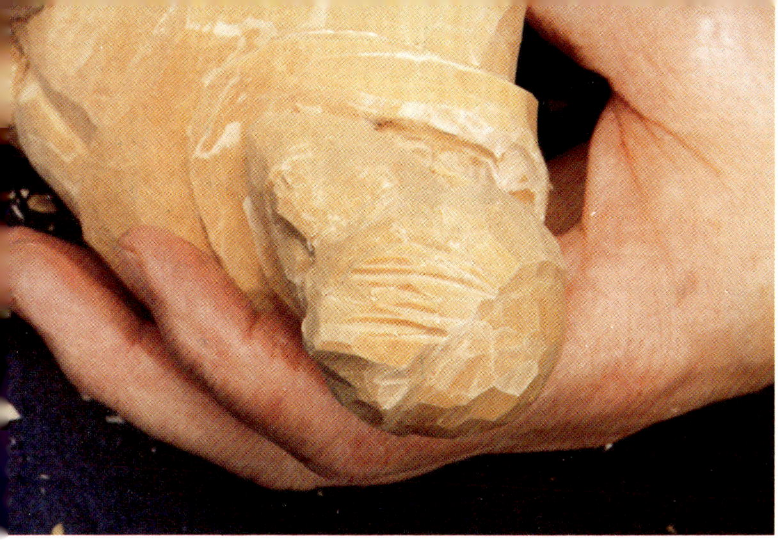

With a V-tool add hair lines to the head.

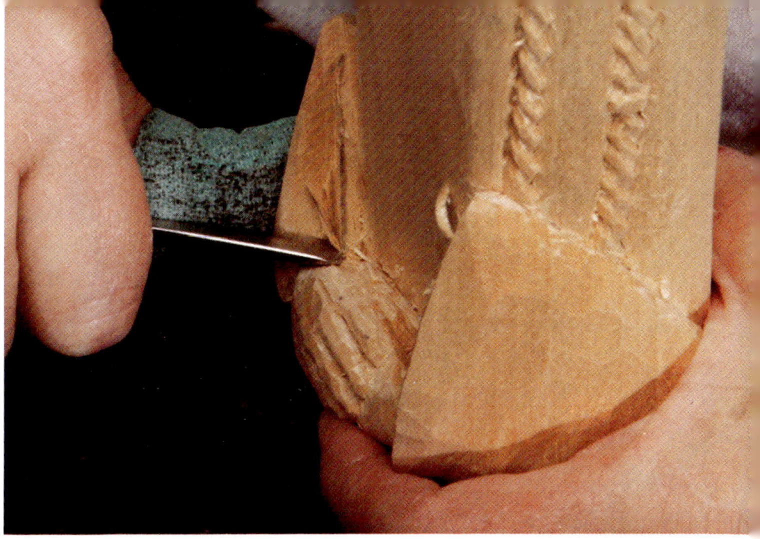

Switch to skew to enlarge the opening.

Draw the opening of the sleeve.

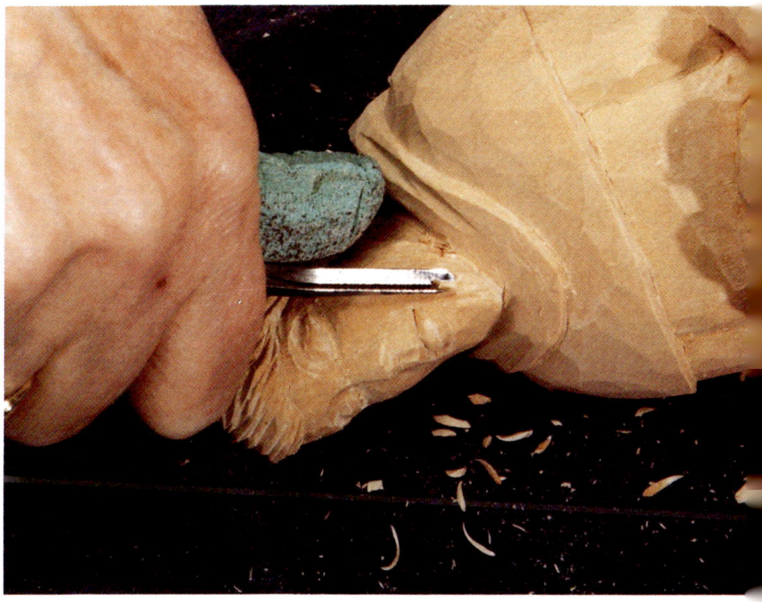

With a V-tool go back and add hair lines to the beard.

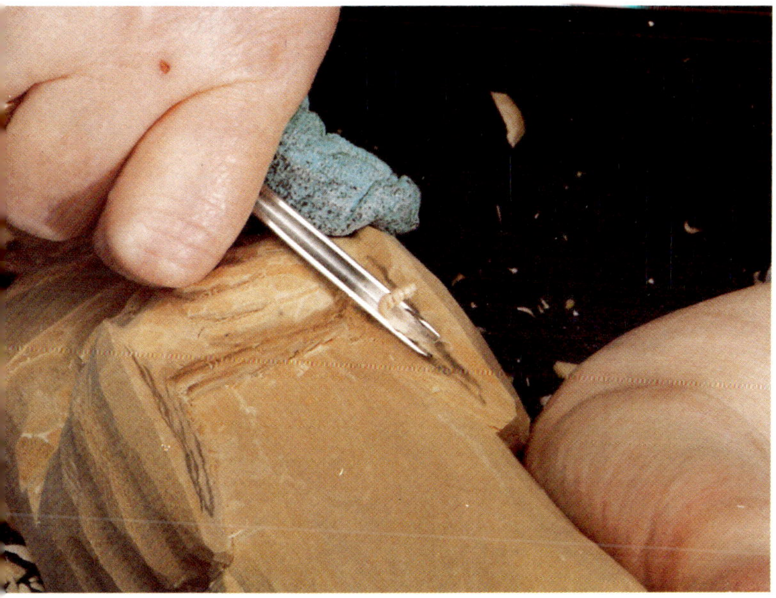

Start removing the sleeve material with a veiner.

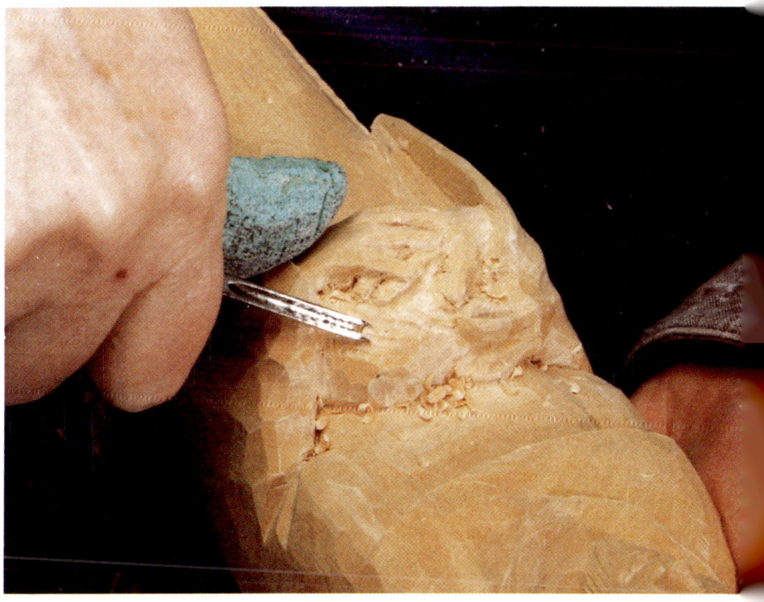

With a small U-shaped gouge, make hair on the rabbit.

Ready for sanding.

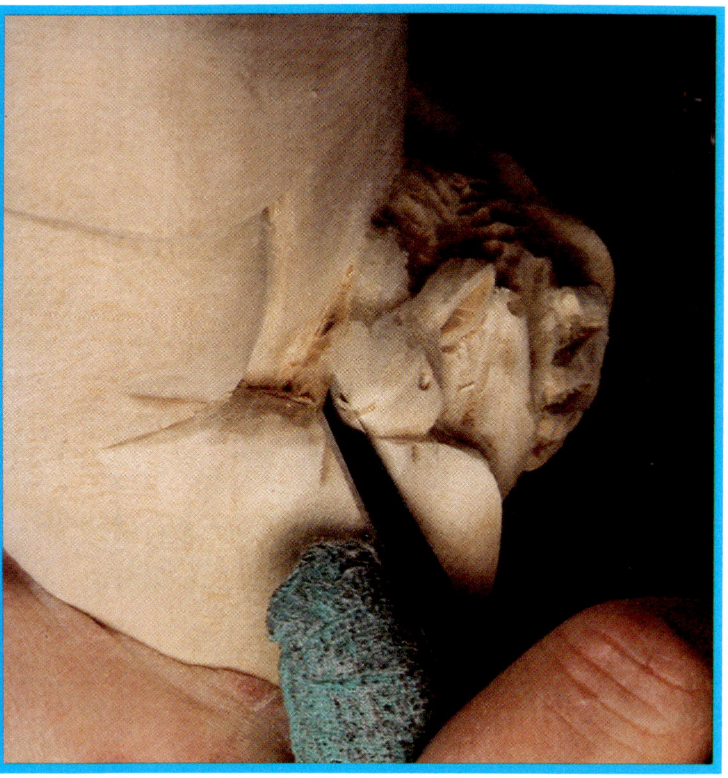

Begin the sanding with 120 grit paper. I use cloth backed paper rolled up into a cylinder.

An X makes the nose and the mouth. Pop out the triangle at the bottom for the mouth.

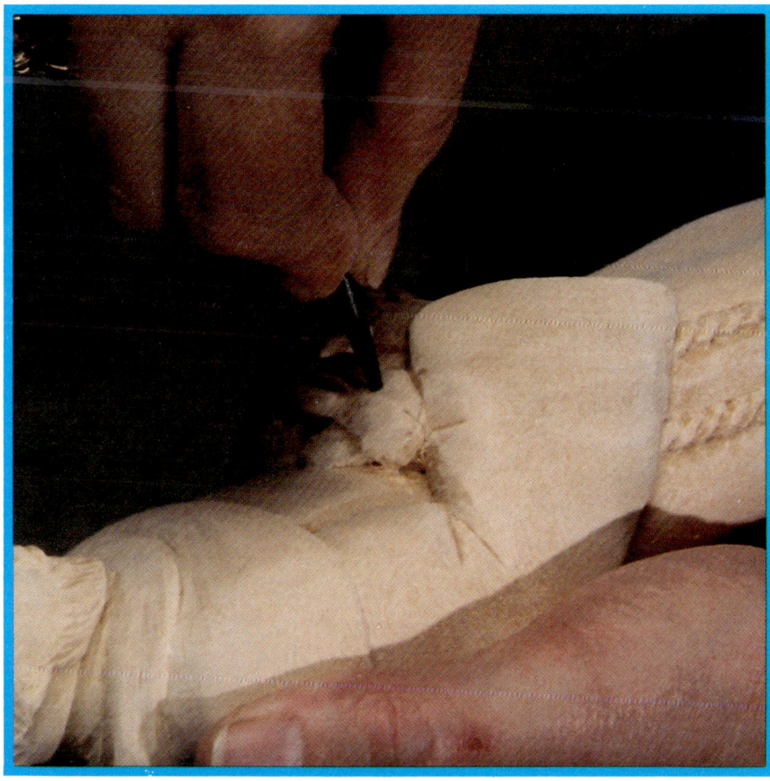

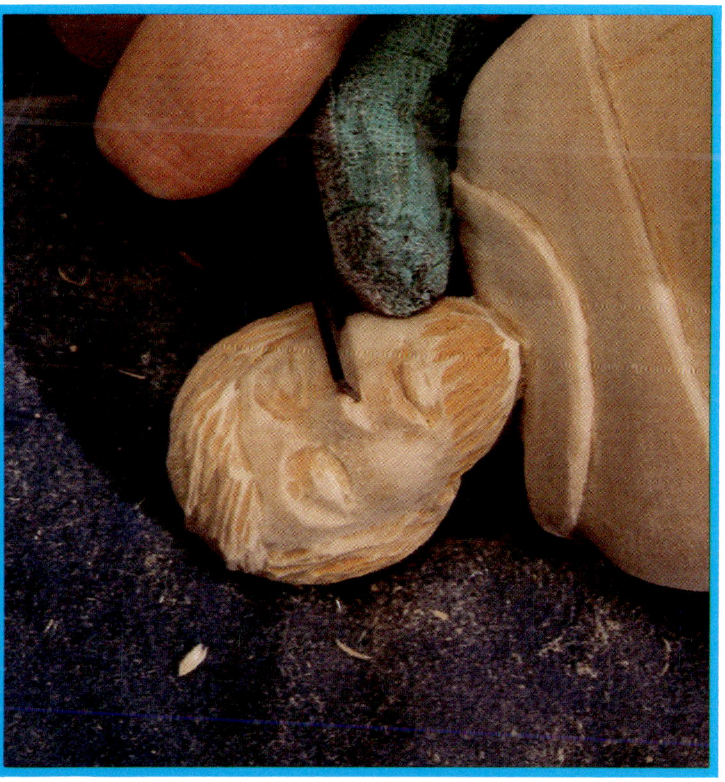

As you begin to sand you are likely to notice things that you have missed. In this carving I forgot some details on the rabbit and on St. Francis's nose. Use an eyepunch or small nail set to create an eye in the rabbit. Simply push in and turn.

I forgot to carve the nostrils on St. Francis, too. A little bit taken with the knife from each side of the nose should do it.

Go over the piece a second time with fine sand paper.

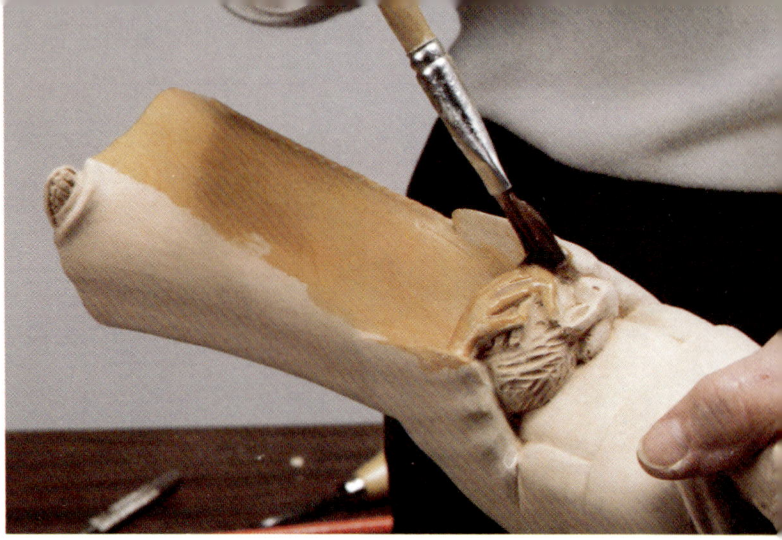

I finish the piece with Deft semi-gloss clear finish.

Create the fingernails by cutting in...

and down.

The first coat applied.

Sand with 220 grit paper when the first coat is completely dry.

Apply a second coat.

Sand again after the second coat.

Apply a third coat.

When it dries buff it with a Scotch Brite™ pad (without soap).

Apply a coat of paste wax or clear shoe polish.

Wait five minutes and buff it with a soft rag.

# Gallery

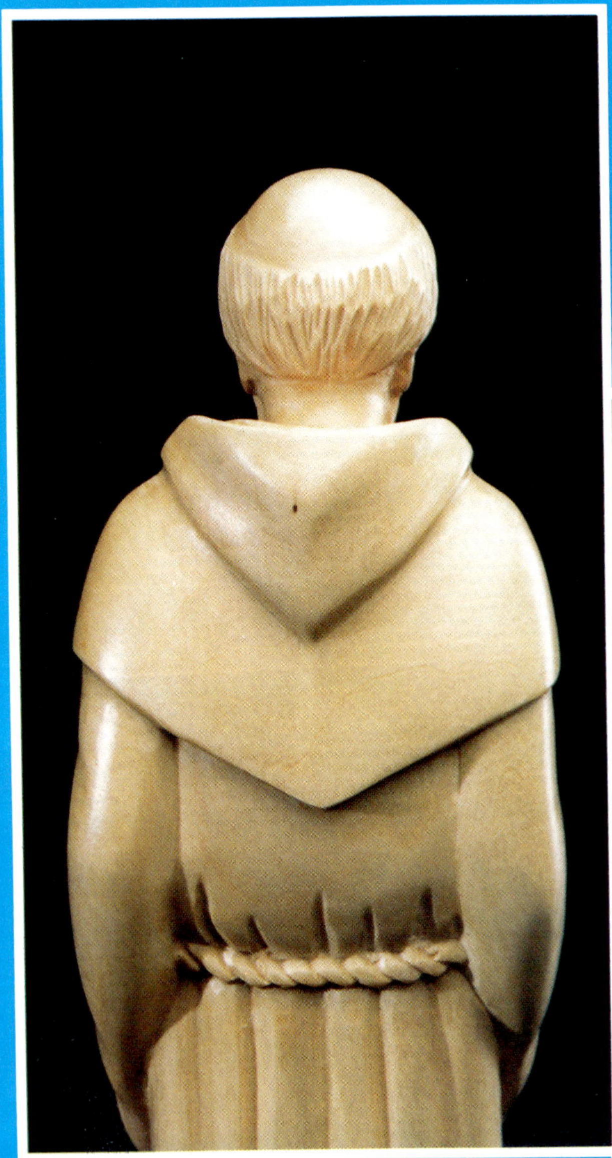

The finished piece.